Learn OpenGL

Beginner's guide to 3D rendering and game development with OpenGL and C++

Frahaan Hussain

BIRMINGHAM - MUMBAI

Learn OpenGL

Copyright © 2018 Packt Publishing

All rights reserved. No part of this book may be reproduced, stored in a retrieval system, or transmitted in any form or by any means, without the prior written permission of the publisher, except in the case of brief quotations embedded in critical articles or reviews.

Every effort has been made in the preparation of this book to ensure the accuracy of the information presented. However, the information contained in this book is sold without warranty, either express or implied. Neither the author, nor Packt Publishing or its dealers and distributors, will be held liable for any damages caused or alleged to have been caused directly or indirectly by this book.

Packt Publishing has endeavored to provide trademark information about all of the companies and products mentioned in this book by the appropriate use of capitals. However, Packt Publishing cannot guarantee the accuracy of this information.

Commissioning Editor: Kunal Chaudhari
Acquisition Editor: Shweta Pant
Content Development Editor: Onkar Wani
Technical Editor: Sachin Sunilkumar
Copy Editor: Safis Editing
Proofreader: Safis Editing
Indexer: Pratik Shirodkar
Graphics: Jason Monteiro
Production Coordinator: Arvindkumar Gupta

First published: August 2018

Production reference: 1310818

Published by Packt Publishing Ltd.
Livery Place
35 Livery Street
Birmingham
B3 2PB, UK.

ISBN 978-1-78934-036-5

www.packtpub.com

`mapt.io`

Mapt is an online digital library that gives you full access to over 5,000 books and videos, as well as industry leading tools to help you plan your personal development and advance your career. For more information, please visit our website.

Why subscribe?

- Spend less time learning and more time coding with practical eBooks and Videos from over 4,000 industry professionals

- Improve your learning with Skill Plans built especially for you

- Get a free eBook or video every month

- Mapt is fully searchable

- Copy and paste, print, and bookmark content

Packt.com

Did you know that Packt offers eBook versions of every book published, with PDF and ePub files available? You can upgrade to the eBook version at `www.packt.com` and as a print book customer, you are entitled to a discount on the eBook copy. Get in touch with us at `customercare@packtpub.com` for more details.

At `www.packt.com`, you can also read a collection of free technical articles, sign up for a range of free newsletters, and receive exclusive discounts and offers on Packt books and eBooks.

Contributors

About the author

Frahaan Hussain is the CEO of Sonar Systems which is the world leader in educational material for the game engine Cocos2d-x, one of the best and the most popular game engines in the world. With years of experience in programming and running an online education platform (Sonar Learning), he enjoys to help and support new programmers like you. He is also a University Lecturer teaching a variety of topics in Games Programming from Games Design to OpenGL Shader Programming.

Packt is searching for authors like you

If you're interested in becoming an author for Packt, please visit `authors.packtpub.com` and apply today. We have worked with thousands of developers and tech professionals, just like you, to help them share their insight with the global tech community. You can make a general application, apply for a specific hot topic that we are recruiting an author for, or submit your own idea.

Table of Contents

Preface   1

Chapter 1: Setting Up OpenGL   7
  Setting up OpenGL using GLFW and GLEW on Windows   8
    Downloading the essential libraries   8
    Linking GLFW and GLEW libraries with absolute linking   11
    Linking GLFW and GLEW libraries with relative linking   16
    Adding a dynamic link library to the project   20
  Setting up OpenGL using GLFW on a Mac   20
    Downloading the GLFW and GLEW libraries for a Mac   21
    Setting up Xcode for OpenGL   22
  Creating the OpenGL rendering window using GLFW   24
  Setting up OpenGL using SDL on Windows   30
    Downloading the SDL library   30
    Setting up OpenGL using SDL and GLEW with absolute linking   31
    Setting up OpenGL using SDL and GLEW with relative linking   32
    Adding a DLL file to the project   35
  Setting up OpenGL using SDL on a Mac   35
    Downloading the SDL and GLEW libraries   35
    Setting up Xcode for OpenGL using SDL   36
  Creating the OpenGL rendering window using SDL   37
  Setting up OpenGL using SFML on Windows   41
    Downloading the SFML library   41
    Linking the SFML and GLEW libraries to the project   41
    Adding a DLL file to the project   41
  Setting up OpenGL using SFML on a Mac   42
  Creating the OpenGL rendering window using SFML   42
  Summary   44

Chapter 2: Drawing Shapes and Applying Textures   45
  Drawing a triangle   46
    Adding code to draw the shape   53
  Abstracting the shaders   55
    Creating the shader files   56
    Creating the Shader.h header file   57
    Making changes to the draw triangle code   60
  Loading and applying textures to the shape   63
    Setting up a project to use SOIL on Windows   64
    Setting up a project to use SOIL on Mac   66
    Applying texture to our shape   67

Modifying the while loop	73
Updating the shader files to integrate texture coordinates	75
Summary	76
Chapter 3: Transformations, Projections, and Camera	**77**
Transformations using GLM	**78**
Setting up a project to use GLM on Windows / Mac	78
Updating shader files	79
Applying transformations to the objects	79
Projections and coordinate systems	**82**
Modifications to the code	83
Making modifications to the shader files	84
Modifications to the main code	85
View Frustum	87
Modifications to while loop	88
Orthgraphic projection	91
Adding a Camera class to the project	**94**
Creating a Camera.h header file	95
Making modifications to main.cpp	103
Summary	**111**
Chapter 4: Effects of lighting , Materials and Lightmaps	**113**
Adding an object and a light source	**114**
Creating lighting and lamp shader files	114
Creating shader files for the lamp	115
Modifying the main code to implement a cube and a light source	116
Modifications to the while loop	118
Lighting up objects	**122**
Updating the shaders	122
What are normals ?	123
Updating the lighting.frag shader	124
Ambient lighting	124
Diffuse lighting	125
Specular lighting	126
Minor change in Camera.h	126
Making changes to the main code	126
Materials	**131**
Updating shader files for Materials	132
Making changes to the main code to add materials to our object	134
Lightmaps	**137**
Making modifications to shader files	138
Changes to the main code to implement lightmaps	141
Modifying while loop	144
Summary	**146**
Chapter 5: Types of light sources and combining of lights	**147**
Directional light	**147**
Directional lights	148

Table of Contents

Making changes to main code to integrate directional light in our world	150
Point lights	**153**
The point light concept	153
The diffuse section	154
The specular section	155
The attenuation section	155
Time for changes in main.cpp	156
Spotlight	**161**
Making changes to shader files	162
Minor modification to Camera.h	164
Making changes to the main code	164
Combining light	**168**
Getting the shader files ready	168
Making modifications void main of lighting.frag	171
Changes to the main code	175
Summary	**182**
Chapter 6: Implementing a Skybox Using a Cubemap	**183**
Creating shaders for the skybox	**184**
Modifications to the main.cpp file	**185**
Creating the Texture.h file	186
Adding cube mapping code to Texture.h	189
Drawing the skybox	190
Summary	**192**
Other Books You May Enjoy	**193**
Index	**197**

[iii]

Preface

OpenGL is the most popular graphics library in the world; most mobile games use OpenGL and many other applications. In this book, you'll get to learn about the fundamentals that make the awesome games we play and the game engines behind them. A step-by-step process is used to show everything, from setting up OpenGL to its essential modern features. You'll gain a good understanding of the following concepts: setting up on Windows and Mac using GLFW, SDL, and SFML, 2D drawing, 3D drawing, texturing, lighting, 3D rendering, Shaders/GLSL, model loading, and cube mapping.

Who this book is for

Learn OpenGL is for anyone and everyone who is interested in creating games, learning how game engines work, and most importantly for anyone who is interested in learning OpenGL. The ideal reader for this book would be anyone with a passion for learning game development or looking out for an OpenGL reference guide. The skills that you'll learn in this book will be applicable to all your game development needs. You'll require a strong foundation in C++ to understand and apply the concepts of this book.

What this book covers

`Chapter 1`, *Setting Up OpenGL*, In this chapter, you'll get to learn how to set up OpenGL using various libraries: GLFW, GLEW, SDL, and SFML. We'll learn how to set up our OpenGL projects on Windows and Mac. We also discuss how to link the libraries to your projects using absolute or relative linking, and eventually create the rendering windows to display OpenGL graphics.

`Chapter 2`, *Drawing Shapes and Applying Textures*, takes you through drawing various shapes using shaders. We'll begin by drawing a triangle and learn to add color to it. Then, we'll use the triangle concept to draw our quadrilateral and also learn how to add texture to it.

`Chapter 3`, *Transformations, Projections, and Camera*, This chapter further builds on the previous chapter. You'll get to grips with applying transformations such as rotation and translation to our shapes, and learn to draw a cube and apply a texture to it. Then, we explore the concepts of projections (perspective and orthographic) and implement those concepts in our game world.

Preface

Chapter 4, *Effects of lighting, Materials, and Lightmaps*, In this chapter we'll learn to apply colors to our objects and how to create a light source such as a lamp in our game world. We'll then look at the effects of light on the objects. You'll understand different types of lighting techniques: ambient, diffused, specular lighting. We'll also explore the various real worl materials and observe the effects of light on the materials. You'll also get to learn about lightmaps in this chapter.

Chapter 5, *Types of light sources and combining of lights*, This chapter will discuss the different types of light sources such as directional lights, point lights, and spotlights. We'll also learn to combine the lighting effects and the light sources for our game world.

Chapter 6, *Implementing a Skybox Using a Cubemap*, In this chapter, you'll generate a skybox using a cubemap. You'll learn how to apply textures to the skybox and then create a separate texture file to make loading of textures in the code easier. You'll also learn to draw the skybox and create our game world using it.

Online Chapter, *Model Loading*, This is a bonus chapter available at https://www.packtpub.com/sites/default/files/downloads/ModelLoading.pdf. In this chapter, you'll learn how to setup Assimp (Open Asset Import Library) on Windows using CMake for all our Model Loading needs. We'll also cover setting up Assimp on Mac OS X and creating a cross-platform Mesh Class. Then we'll explore how to load a 3D model into our game. You'll also get to learn how to create a Model Class to handle loading of our model.

To get the most out of this book

For this book, it's really important that you have a good foundation in C++ as in this book you will be using OpenGL with C++. It's not the easiest thing, OpenGL. If this is your first time coding or you haven't been coding for long, it is recommended you get a good grasp of C++ and then continue with the book.

Disclaimer

The illustrations used in this book are for illustrative purposes only. We do not recommend you to misuse these in any way. For more information please consult the terms and conditions of the publishers mentioned here.

Nintendo : https://www.nintendo.com/terms-of-use

Download the example code files

You can download the example code files for this book from your account at www.packt.com. If you purchased this book elsewhere, you can visit www.packt.com/support and register to have the files emailed directly to you.

You can download the code files by following these steps:

1. Log in or register at www.packt.com.
2. Select the **SUPPORT** tab.
3. Click on **Code Downloads & Errata**.
4. Enter the name of the book in the **Search** box and follow the onscreen instructions.

Once the file is downloaded, please make sure that you unzip or extract the folder using the latest version of:

- WinRAR/7-Zip for Windows
- Zipeg/iZip/UnRarX for Mac
- 7-Zip/PeaZip for Linux

The code bundle for the book is also hosted on GitHub at https://github.com/PacktPublishing/Learn-OpenGL. In case there's an update to the code, it will be updated on the existing GitHub repository.

We also have other code bundles from our rich catalog of books and videos available at https://github.com/PacktPublishing/. Check them out!

Download the color images

We also provide a PDF file that has color images of the screenshots/diagrams used in this book. You can download it here: https://www.packtpub.com/sites/default/files/downloads/LearnOpenGL_ColorImages.pdf.

Conventions used

There are a number of text conventions used throughout this book.

`CodeInText`: Indicates code words in text, database table names, folder names, filenames, file extensions, pathnames, dummy URLs, user input, and Twitter handles. Here is an example: "Extract the library files for GLEW and GLFW in `External Libraries` folder."

A block of code is set as follows:

```
SDL_GL_SetAttribute(SDL_GL_CONTEXT_MAJOR_VERSION, 3);
SDL_GL_SetAttribute(SDL_GL_CONTEXT_MINOR_VERSION, 3);
SDL_GL_SetAttribute(SDL_GL_STENCIL_SIZE, 8);
```

When we wish to draw your attention to a particular part of a code block, the relevant lines or items are set in bold:

```
SDL_GL_SetAttribute(SDL_GL_CONTEXT_MAJOR_VERSION, 3);
SDL_GL_SetAttribute(SDL_GL_CONTEXT_MINOR_VERSION, 3);
SDL_GL_SetAttribute(SDL_GL_STENCIL_SIZE, 8);
```

Any command-line input or output is written as follows:

```
brew install glfw3
brew install glew
```

Bold: Indicates a new term, an important word, or words that you see onscreen. For example, words in menus or dialog boxes appear in the text like this. Here is an example: "Open up Xcode and click on the **Create a new Xcode project** option."

Warnings or important notes appear like this.

Tips and tricks appear like this.

Get in touch

Feedback from our readers is always welcome.

General feedback: If you have questions about any aspect of this book, mention the book title in the subject of your message and email us at `customercare@packtpub.com`.

Errata: Although we have taken every care to ensure the accuracy of our content, mistakes do happen. If you have found a mistake in this book, we would be grateful if you would report this to us. Please visit `www.packt.com/submit-errata`, selecting your book, clicking on the Errata Submission Form link, and entering the details.

Piracy: If you come across any illegal copies of our works in any form on the Internet, we would be grateful if you would provide us with the location address or website name. Please contact us at `copyright@packt.com` with a link to the material.

If you are interested in becoming an author: If there is a topic that you have expertise in and you are interested in either writing or contributing to a book, please visit `authors.packtpub.com`.

Reviews

Please leave a review. Once you have read and used this book, why not leave a review on the site that you purchased it from? Potential readers can then see and use your unbiased opinion to make purchase decisions, we at Packt can understand what you think about our products, and our authors can see your feedback on their book. Thank you!

For more information about Packt, please visit `packt.com`.

Setting Up OpenGL

Welcome to the world of modern OpenGL. **Open Graphics Library (OpenGL)** is an API that provides developers with various sets of functions that enable them to manipulate graphics and images. It is the core framework of most games today, whether it's mobile games for iOS or Android, or for other platforms, such as desktops and consoles as well. OpenGL just speaks for itself. Take a look at any sort of game you can think of, and it is doable in OpenGL. It's not just restricted to 3D; you can create 2D games as well. The 2D and 3D game engines are created using OpenGL, so it is more than capable of anything that you can think of. In this book, we will learn all the concepts necessary for 3D game development.

In this chapter, we'll take a look at how to set up OpenGL on Windows and Mac, using various libraries, such as GLFW, GLEW, SDL, and SFML. Our main focus for this chapter will be to understand how to download the libraries and set up OpenGL using those. While we are learning about how to set up our projects, we will also take a look at how to link these libraries to our project using absolute and relative linking.

The following topics will be covered in this chapter:

- Downloading the essential libraries
- Setting up a project on different platforms to use the libraries
- Creating an OpenGL rendering window using the libraries

You can refer to all the code files for this chapter in the Chapter01 folder on GitHub. The GitHub link can be found in the preface of the book.

Setting up OpenGL using GLFW and GLEW on Windows

In this section, we'll learn how to set up OpenGL using GLFW and GLEW on your Windows system, by using Visual Studio. But, first let's understand what GLFW and GLEW are. **GLFW** is an **OpenGL framework**. It's a very lightweight framework that allows us to detect events such as keyboard input, mouse input, and other sort of inputs, but more importantly, it allows you to create a render window in which you can render your code, as OpenGL doesn't have a way of creating a rendering window, and it needs something like GLFW to create it.

GLEW is the **OpenGL Extension Wrangler,** which basically allows you to use OpenGL functions that are new, or more precisely, non-core. It provides systematic mechanisms during runtime to determine which OpenGL extensions are supported on the target platform. For any new functions, you essentially require something like OpenGL Extension Wrangler to initialize extensions and to write portable applications.

First things first: For this book, it's really important that you have a good foundation in C++, as, in this book, you will be using OpenGL with C++. It's not the easiest thing, OpenGL. If this is your first time coding or you haven't been coding for long, it is recommended you get a good grasp of C++ and then continue with the book.

Let's begin our setup process by downloading the GLFW and GLEW libraries.

Downloading the essential libraries

Let's get started with the setup, by performing below mentioned steps:

1. First of all, we will need Visual Studio. You might have already installed it. If you did, it's fantastic. If not, go to `https://visualstudio.microsoft.com/`, go to **Downloads**, and then click to download the **Visual Studio Community 2017** version. Then, follow the instructions and install Visual Studio onto your system. Once you've got that installed, you just want to make sure it's set up for the C++ environment.

If you have the *Pro* version, that's fantastic, but the *Community* version will more than suffice.

Chapter 1

2. Next, we will download the **OpenGL Extension Wrangler** library. Visit `http://glew.sourceforge.net/`, and then click on the **Binaries** option to download the 32-bit or 64-bit version files, as per your system requirements:

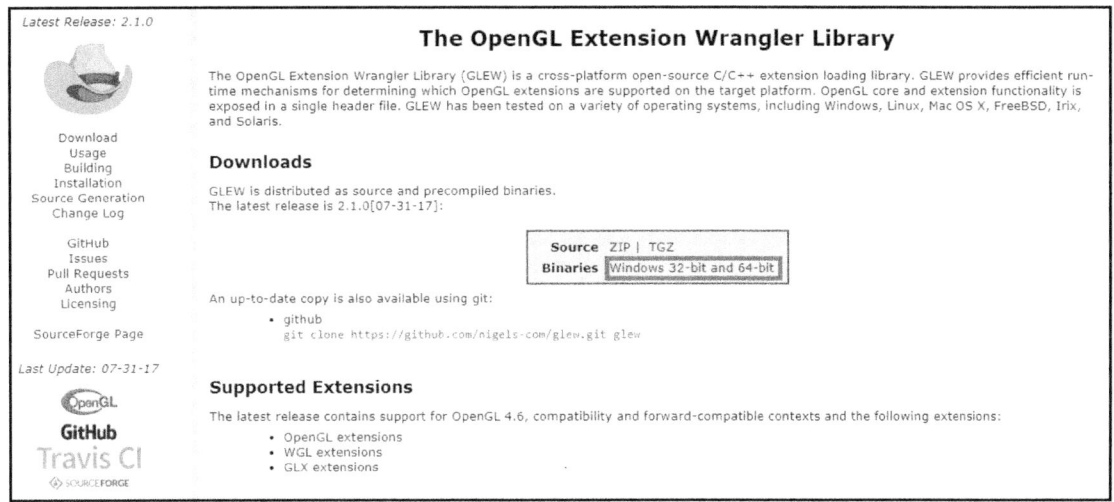

Downloading binaries for GLEW

After downloading, just unzip the file and put it somewhere you find feasible to access, because for this project, and any other projects that you create, it will reference that directory. So, you don't want to be moving it around because then you will have to redo the settings for your project. For this project, it's recommended that you create a folder called `OpenGL` in your `C:` drive and place all the downloaded libraries in it. This will help you with easy access to the libraries while you are linking those to your project.

When you extract the files, they won't be named nicely and you might find it confusing to view with all the version numbers and stuff. Therefore, to take off any versioning text, it's better that you rename the folders to something as simple as `GLEW` and `GLFW`. It's neat this way, you can easily know what you're doing, and it makes it a lot easier to see things.

[9]

Setting Up OpenGL

3. Once you have done that, we will move on to downloading **OpenGL framework library files.** Go to `http://www.glfw.org/` and click on the **Download** menu. We will want to download the precompiled binaries for Windows. As seen in the following screenshot, select and click to download either the 32-bit or 64-bit version as per your system requirements:

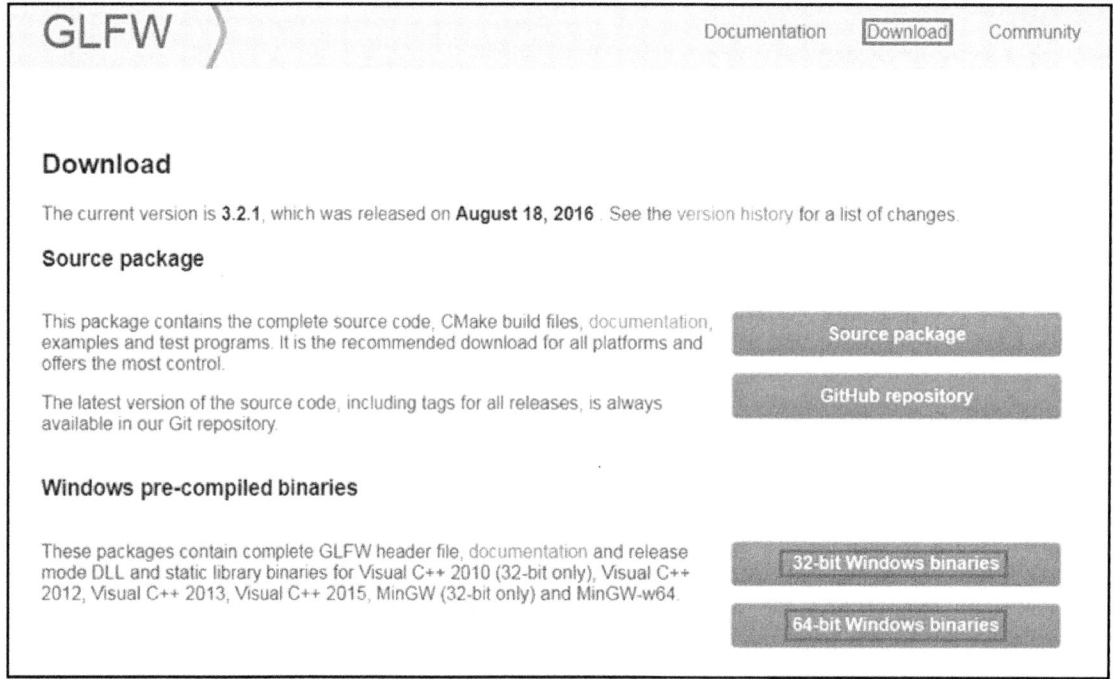

Downloading binaries for GLFW

Note: Even if you know you need to download the 64-bit version for developing on a 64-bit machine, try to stick with the 32-bit version, because unless you think your game or your application is going to be using more than 4 GB of memory, the 32- bit version will more than suffice and it will help you in maximizing compatibility.

Once you've downloaded the file, unzip it and, as mentioned before, place it in the `GLFW` folder inside the `OpenGL` folder.

Chapter 1

Linking GLFW and GLEW libraries with absolute linking

After we have downloaded all the necessary files, we will set up the environment in Visual Studio for OpenGL using the GLFW and GLEW libraries. Follow these steps:

1. Open Visual Studio, and then click on **Create new Project...**:

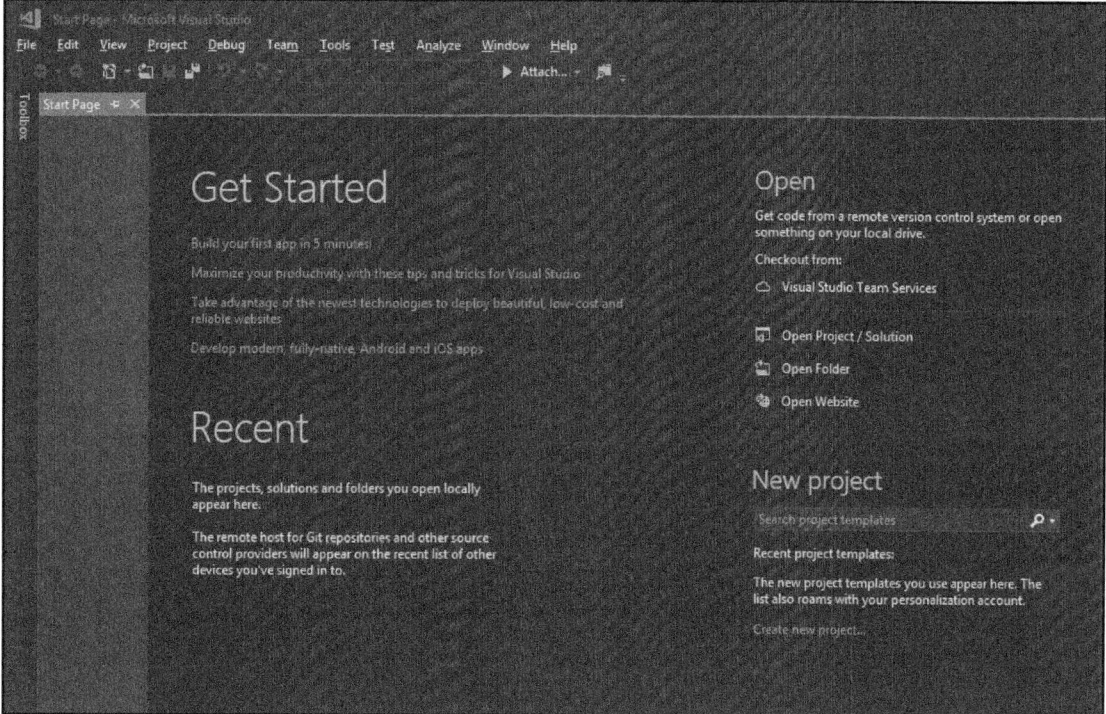

Visual Studio start page

Setting Up OpenGL

2. Then, go to **Visual C++ | Windows Desktop | Windows Console Application** and name your project `GLFWOpenGL`, as seen in the following screenshot, and then click **OK**:

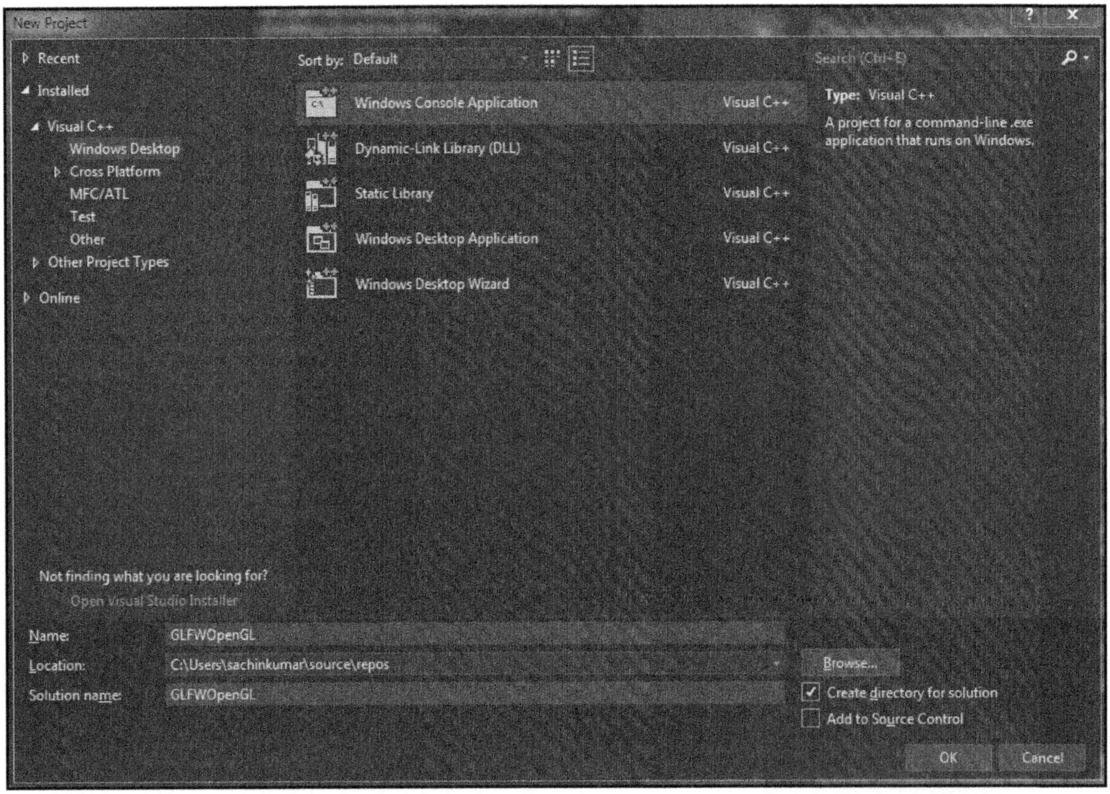

Creating a new project

 If you don't see the **Visual C++** option in the **New Project** window, you might need to download Visual C++. For more information, you can visit the following link: https://docs.microsoft.com/en-us/cpp/build/vscpp-step-0-installation

3. Now, right-click on the project in the **Solution Explorer** window. Go to **Add | New Item**, and you will get an **Add New Item** window. Select **C++ File**, as this will be our main file, and let's name it `main.cpp` and then click on the **Add** button.

[12]

Chapter 1

4. Next, right-click on the project in the **Solution Explorer** window. Click on **Properties**.
5. A **Property Pages** window will pop up; click on **C/C++ | General** and then go to **Additional Include Directories**. Click on the dropdown, then click on **<Edit>**, and you will get a pop up window as follows:

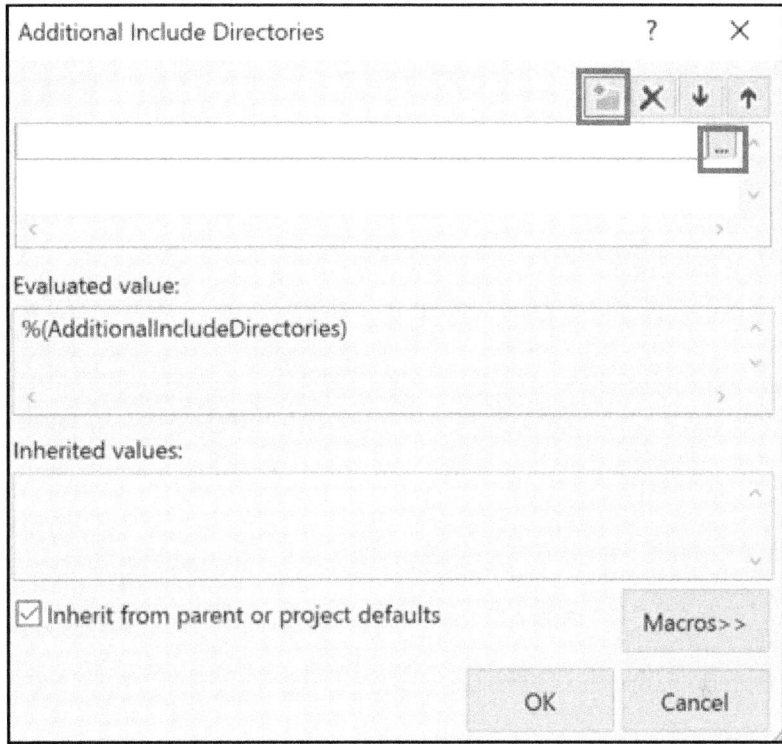

Adding include directories

6. As highlighted in the preceding screenshot, click on the new button and then click on the three dots. And now, browse to the GLEW folder inside the OpenGL folder. Select the include folder and then click on the **Select Folder** button. Next, we repeat the same process to add the GLFW library to our project. Once we have included both the libraries, click on the **OK** button.

Setting Up OpenGL

7. Now, again in the **Property Pages** window, we'll go to **Linker | General**, and then go to **Additional Library Directories**. Click on the dropdown, then click on <Edit>, and you will get a pop-up window, as follows:

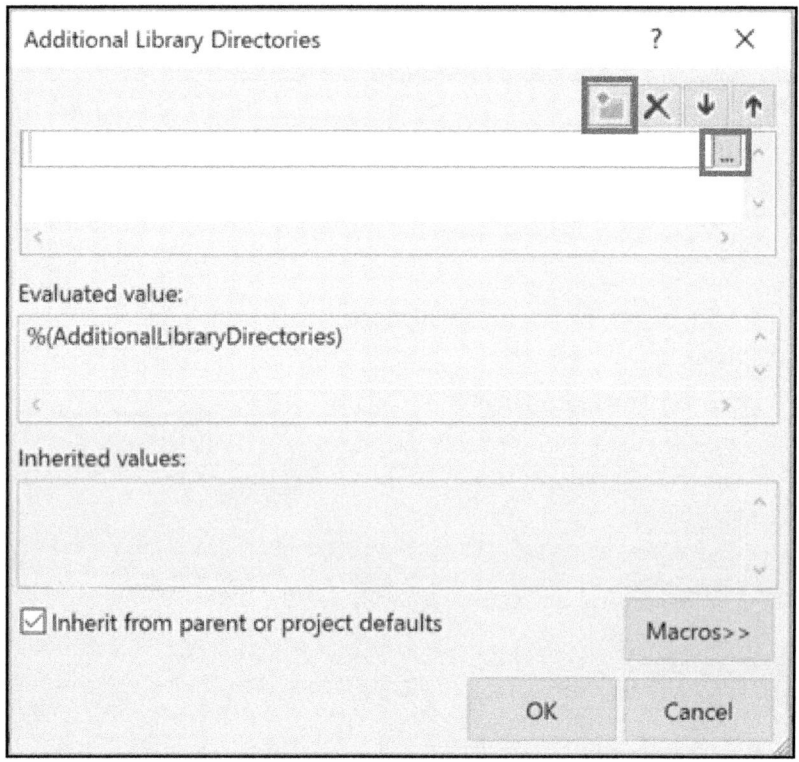

Adding libraries

8. As highlighted in the preceding screenshot, click on the new button and then click on the three dots. Now, browse to the OpenGL folder where you have downloaded the GLEW files. Open the lib folder inside the GLEW folder, then double-click on the Release folder, select Win32, and then click on the **Select Folder** button.
9. Repeat the same process to include GLFW libraries. But for GLFW, you've got a bunch of different libraries that you could choose from. For our project, it's best that we select the lib-vc2015 folder. Once you have added both the libraries, click on the **OK** button.

Chapter 1

There are a bunch of other versions of libraries that you can choose for GLFW. So, if you have an older version of Visual Studio, you can select the library for that particular version.

10. Next, we'll go to **Linker | Input**, and then go to **Additional Dependencies.** Click on the dropdown, and then click on **Edit**. What we'll do here is type `opengl32.lib` in the textbox, as seen highlighted in the following screenshot. `opengl32.lib` is the library built into the operating system. Next, we'll type `glew32s.lib`. This is the static library and it will be statically linked to your project. If you don't want to statically link it, you can just remove the `s` from the suffix; it is up to you. Next, we'll type `glfw3.lib`, and then click on the **OK** button:

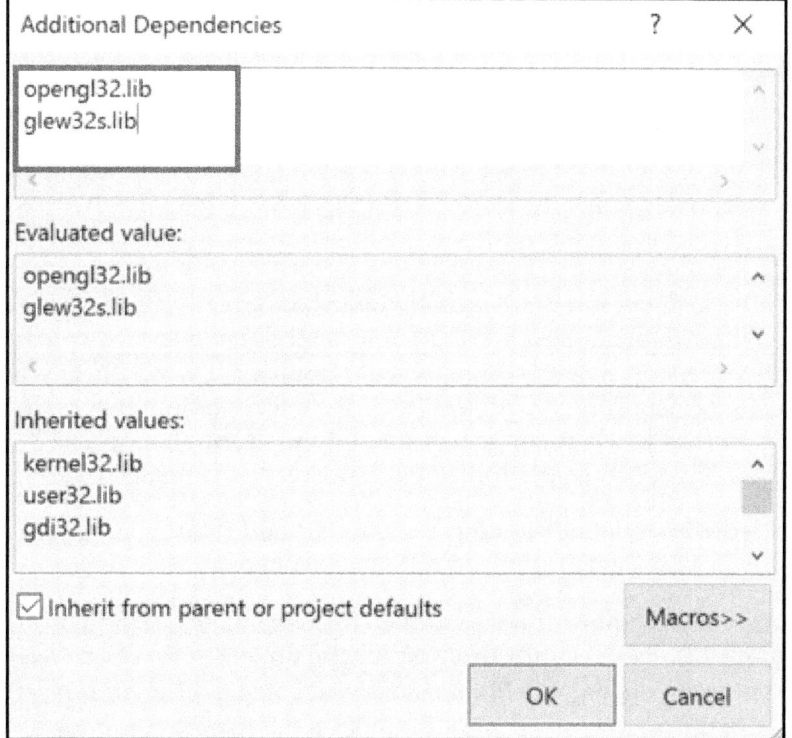

Adding additional dependencies

11. Then, click on the **Apply** button.

[15]

In the preceding section, we discussed how to download the essential libraries and how to link them up to our project with absolute linking.

In the following section, we'll study how to link these libraries to our project with relative linking, and we'll also learn about how relative linking is beneficial for us. You can use either one of them to link the libraries to your project; it's your choice.

Linking GLFW and GLEW libraries with relative linking

In this section, we'll take a look at how to set up OpenGL using GLFW as the provider to create a render window with relative linking. In the previous section, we discussed absolute linking, So, let's just have a quick overview of what absolute and relative linking actually are.

Absolute linking is a process where you specifically link your libraries to the project. For example, if you create a project and you are linking up libraries like GLFW and GLEW, while linking them up, you specifically put in the paths of the directory they are in. If they're in the C: drive, you would actually put the explicit directory. But, if you move the library files to any other location, then you would have to update your Visual Studio project with the changed path.

With relative linking, the libraries are actually linked, but relative to the project. So, you don't say libraries are in the C: drive; rather, you say those relatively link to your project from a particular folder. So even if you move your libraries, it won't affect your project. It is a great method for transporting the project from one machine to an other. This method of development is preferable when you're working on a platform that doesn't really have a good visual editor; for example, platforms, such as Unity or Unreal.

So, let's get started with relatively linking our libraries and creating an OpenGL render window. Let's open up Visual Studio and follow these steps:

1. Click on **Create new project...** and go to **Visual C++ | Windows Desktop | Windows Console Application**. Name the project GLApp (since we are learning how to relatively link the libraries, we've created a different project).
2. Then, in the **New Project** window, click on the **Browse...** button. Go to the OpenGL folder that we've created on the desktop (we are using this folder structure format to understand relative linking). Just select the folder and then click **OK**.

Chapter 1

3. One more thing you need to do before starting the project is to create a folder called `External Libraries` within the `OpenGL` folder on desktop where you have saved your project. Extract the library files for GLEW and GLFW in the `External Libraries` folder.

4. Now, we'll right-click on the project in the **Solution Explorer** window. Go to **Add** | **New Item**. Select **C++ File** and name it `main.cpp`, and then click on the **Add** button.

5. Next, right-click on the project in the **Solution Explorer** window and go to **Properties**.

6. A **Property Pages** window will pop up; click on **C/C++** | **General** and then go to **Additional Include Directories**. In it, click on the dropdown and then click on <Edit>:

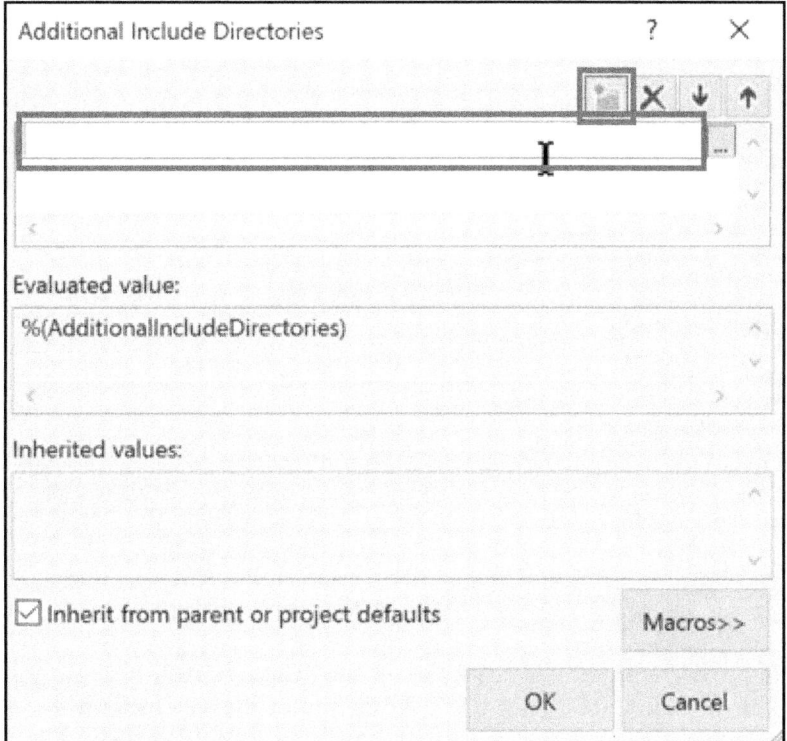

Adding include directories

[17]

Setting Up OpenGL

7. Then, click on the new button. As we are doing relative linking in this section, we won't click on the three dots. Clicking on them is for absolute linking only, as we have to browse to the directory where we have stored the libraries.
8. In the textbox highlighted in the preceding screenshot, type `$(SolutionDir);` this command refers to the folder that contains our `.sln` file. So if we were to specify a folder in the path, whenever we do something new in the project it'd be relatively linked to wherever that file is located.
9. To include the files in our project, add the paths as shown in the following screenshot and then click on the **OK** button:

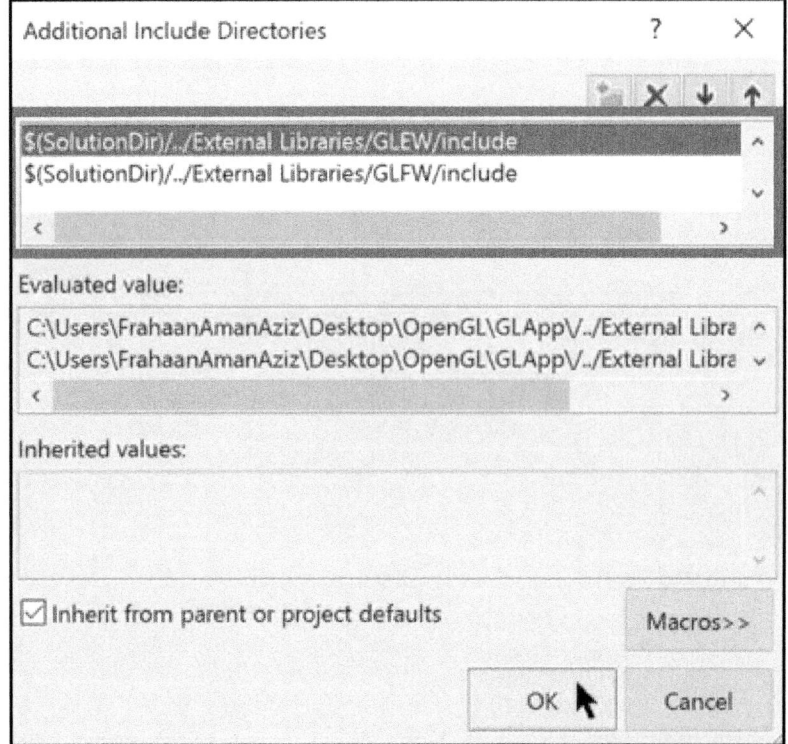

10. Next, we'll link up the libraries. So, in the **Property Pages** window, we'll go to **Linker | General**, and then go to **Additional Library Directories**. Click on the dropdown, click on **Edit**, and then click on **New**. Add the paths as shown in the following screenshot, and then click **OK** and then **Apply**:

Chapter 1

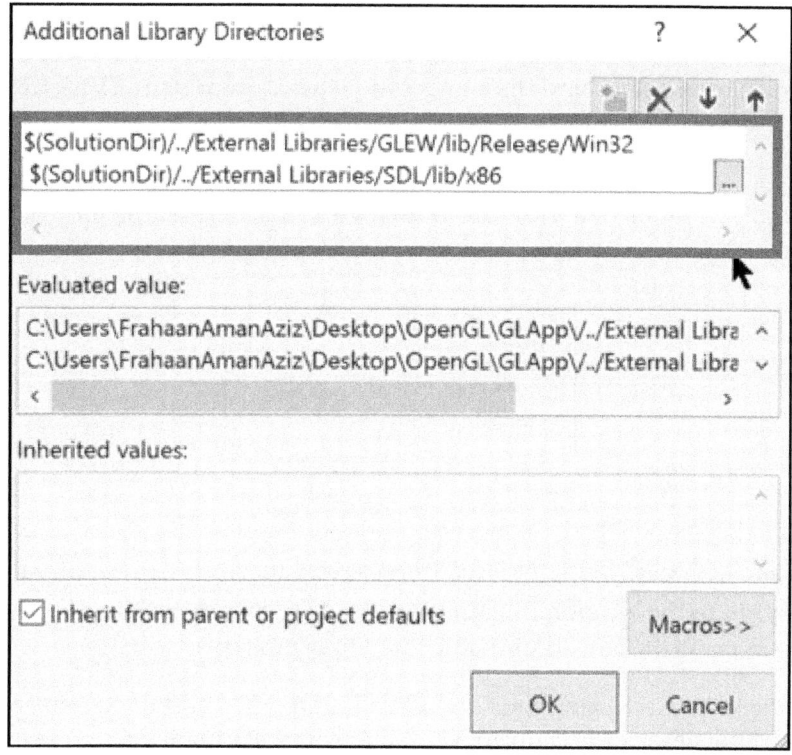

11. Now, we've got one more thing to do, and that is to link up the `.lib` files. So, go to **Linker | Input**, and then go to **Additional Dependencies**. Click on the dropdown and then click on **<Edit>**. Now, in the textbox, just type `opengl32.lib`. This library file isn't downloaded with `GLFW` or `GLEW`; it's built into Windows. Next, on a new line, just type `glew32s.lib` and now for `GLFW` `lib-vc2015`, type `glfw3.lib`. Then, click **OK** and click on the **Apply** button.

Whichever linking process you are comfortable with, you can follow that. With either of the methods that you use to link the libraries, there's one last step that we need complete before we can begin with coding, and that is to copy and paste the dynamic link library into our project.

Setting Up OpenGL

Adding a dynamic link library to the project

Let's take a look at these steps and understand how to add a **dynamic link library (dll)** to our project:

1. Go to the `OpenGL` folder on the `C:` drive; in it, go to the `GLEW` folder, open it and go to `bin`, double-click on it, and then go to `Win32` and open it. Then, copy the `glew32.dll` dynamic link library, as highlighted in the following screenshot:

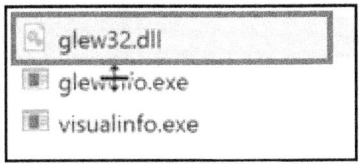

glew32.dll dynamic link library

2. Do as mentioned in the previous step to add the GLFW `.dll` files to your project
3. Now, go to the location in your system where the `main.cpp` file of your project is, and paste the copied dynamic link library file there.

With this last step, we have completed the setup for OpenGL and have also absolutely or relatively linked the libraries to our project. We are now ready to write code for the OpenGL rendering window.

In the preceding section, we discussed how to set up OpenGL on a Windows platform. But, what if any of you are working on a Mac system? Therefore, let's check out how we can download the libraries and set up OpenGL on the Mac platform.

Setting up OpenGL using GLFW on a Mac

Here's what we've discussed so far, we discussed about how to set up our project to use GLFW library on Windows. In this section, we'll discuss how to set up OpenGL on a Mac system. So, let's get started.

Downloading the GLFW and GLEW libraries for a Mac

To download and install the essential libraries onto your Mac system, we'll have to install a package manager for Mac known as **Homebrew**. Homebrew will help us in installing all the necessary packages and libraries to run our OpenGL code.

To install Homebrew, go to `https://brew.sh/`, copy the path highlighted in the following screenshot, paste it into your Terminal, and then hit *Enter*. The prompt will download and install Homebrew on your system:

Path on Homebrew homepage

Setting Up OpenGL

Once we've installed Homebrew, we'll download the GLFW and GLEW libraries onto our system. Let's install GLFW first. To do that, we need to type the following command in the Terminal window:

```
brew install glfw3
```

In the preceding command, you must have observed we've included the number 3; the reason for that is that if you just type `glfw`, it installs an older version, which we don't want, so inserting `glfw3` will install the latest version. Hit *Enter* and the libraries will be downloaded onto your system.

Now, we're going to do the same process for GLEW; type the following command in the Terminal:

```
brew install glew
```

We don't need to put any version for this; just press *Enter* and the necessary files will be downloaded. That's it for the libraries to download onto our system.

Make a note that, since we're installing the libraries on the system itself and not in our project, whenever you move your project to a different system, you will have to install these libraries onto that particular system.

Once we've downloaded and installed all the essential libraries with the help of Homebrew, we'll now move on to setting up Xcode for OpenGL.

Make sure Xcode is installed on to your system. If not, please follow these instructions and install it on your system.

Setting up Xcode for OpenGL

In this section, we'll discuss how to set up Xcode to run our OpenGL code. Follow these steps and carry out the setup process:

1. Open up Xcode and click on the **Create a new Xcode project** option.
2. Go to **OS X | Application**, select **Command Line Tool**, and then click **Next**.
3. You will get the following window; fill in the necessary details, as highlighted in the following screenshot:

[22]

Chapter 1

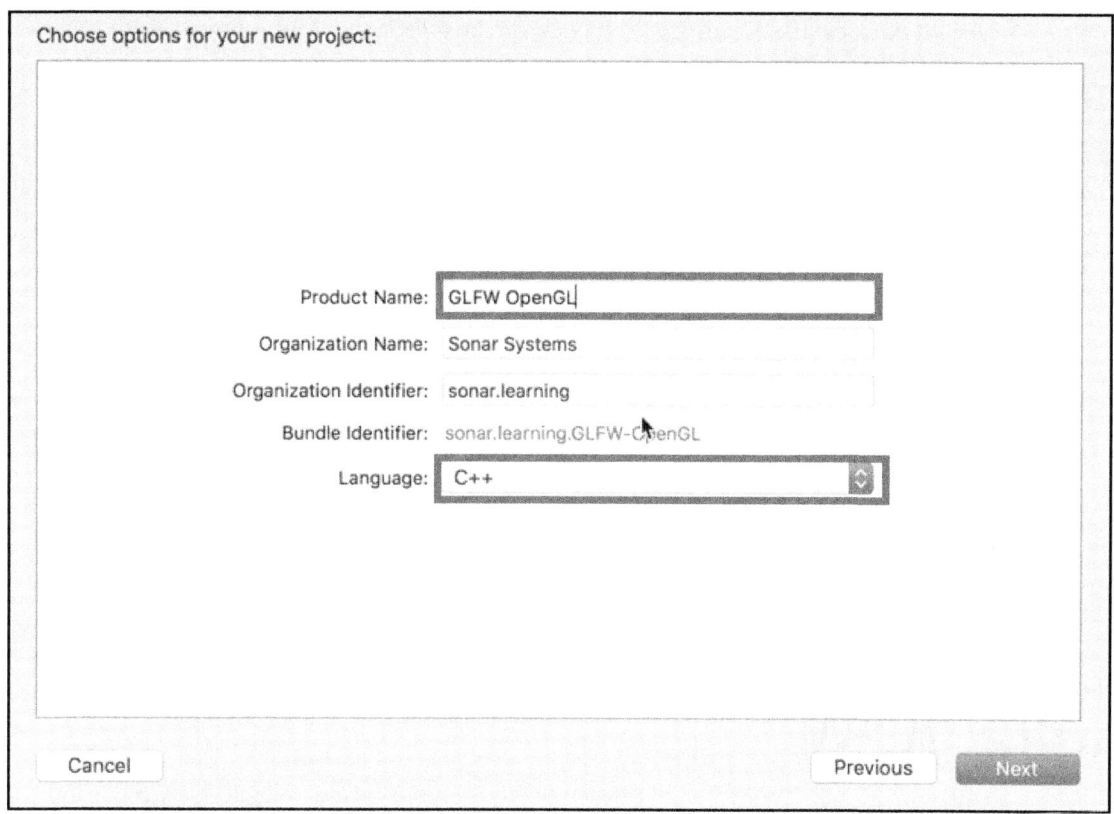

Basic details for a project

4. In the preceding screenshot, make sure that the **Language** option is always set to **C++**, and then click **Next**. The **Organization Name** and **Organization identifier** properties, you can set to whatever you want.
5. Next, set the location you would like to store and save the project to. Then, click on the **Create** button. Next, we have just a plain C++ project ready. Before we begin with our code, we need to follow a few more steps necessary to set up our project.
6. First of all, in Xcode, click on your project and go to **Build Settings**. In **Build Settings**, go to the **Search Paths** section and click on **Header Search Paths**.Then, click on **+** and type `/usr/local/include`. This will allow us to `#include` GLEW and GLFW in our `main.cpp` file.
7. Now go to **Build Phases**, then click on **Link Binary With Libraries**, and click the **+** button. Type `opengl` in the search bar, select **OpenGL.framework**, and then click on the **Add** button.

Setting Up OpenGL

8. Again click on the **+** button, then click on **Add Other....** Now, press *Cmd + Shift + G*, and it will open up a `go-to` folder search bar. In it, type `/usr/local`. Then click on **Cellar**, go to the **glew | lib** folder, select `libGLEW.1.12.0.dylib` without the little arrow, and then click **Open.**

> The arrow is just a shortcut, an alias, and we don't want that. We also don't want the MX version, just the regular `.dy` non-alias lib.

9. Click **+** again, then click **Add Other...** , press *Cmd + Shift + G*, and type `/usr/local`. Now go to **Cellar**, and go to **glfw | lib**. Select the non-alias `libglfw3.3.1.dylib` and click **Open**.

With all the steps executed, our project is now set up to use GLEW and GLFW with OpenGL on Mac. We can now go to the `main.cpp` file on Xcode and start writing our code for creating the OpenGL rendering window.

Creating the OpenGL rendering window using GLFW

Let's go to our `main.cpp` file in Visual Studio or Xcode, and let's get started. Start typing the following code in your editor:

1. Begin by adding some header files to our code:

   ```
   #include <iostream>

   // GLEW
   #define GLEW_STATIC
   #include <GL/glew.h>

   // GLFW
   #include <GLFW/glfw3.h>
   ```

   `iostream` is just the input/output stream built into C++. Then, with `GLEW_STATIC`, we statically linked GLEW. If you don't want to statically link it, just omit the `#define` line.

[24]

2. Next, we'll create some constants, and these will be used to store the width and height of our window:

   ```
   // Window dimensions
   const GLint WIDTH = 800, HEIGHT = 600;
   ```

   You might be thinking, why are we using `GLint` instead of a regular `int`? The reason for that is the issues with a regular `int` on different operating systems; for example, in a different compiler, it might have a different length. With `GLint`, it is consistent on any compiler, so this is a great way of ensuring maximum compatibility.

3. Now, we'll set up our main entry point with `int main` and then we'll initialize GLFW:

   ```
   // The MAIN function, from here we start the application and run
   the game loop
   int main()
   {
       // Init GLFW
       glfwInit();
   ```

4. Next, we'll set up some window hints, which are essentially some properties that we'll set for our window:

   ```
   // Set all the required options for GLFW
   glfwWindowHint(GLFW_CONTEXT_VERSION_MAJOR, 3);
   glfwWindowHint(GLFW_CONTEXT_VERSION_MINOR, 3);
   ```

   The reason we choose 3.3 is because after version 3.1, the code was deprecated in the old version of OpenGL. This was done to prohibit developers from using the older version of OpenGL. Since 3.3, the OpenGL version matches the shader version. So for 3.3, the OpenGL shader language version is also 3.3; it helps in keeping things consistent, neat, and tidy. But if you need a new feature, feel free to use something like 4.3.

5. Next, we'll type in some more window hints:

   ```
   glfwWindowHint(GLFW_OPENGL_PROFILE, GLFW_OPENGL_CORE_PROFILE);
   ```

Setting Up OpenGL

In this project, we'll be using `CORE_PROFILE`. Actually, there are two main profiles that are available: the core profile and the compatibility profile, `COMPAT_PROFILE`. The reason we are using `CORE_PROFILE` in our project is that `CORE_PROFILE` uses the new OpenGL stuff, whereas the compatibility profile uses the old way of doing things, thus ensuring maximum compatibility. You probably might be thinking even if it ensures maximum compatibility, why is it recommended not to use `COMPAT_PROFILE`? The reason for that is in this book you're learning OpenGL in general, so we don't want to learn the old, outdated way of doing things. Rather, we want to learn the new, modern OpenGL using vertex objects and vertex arrays to actually store stuff on a graphics card. So if you use the compatibility mode, you're just getting into bad practices when using stuff like `glBegin`. So, that is the reason why we are setting it to the core profile.

6. Once we've set the profile, we set the window hint to get forward compatibility:

    ```
    glfwWindowHint(GLFW_OPENGL_FORWARD_COMPAT, GL_TRUE);
    ```

    This window hint is actually required in macOS because otherwise it will crash, but there's no harm in having it on Windows as well.

7. In `WindowHint`, we'll set `GLFW_RESIZABLE`, and we'll set this to `FALSE` so that it prevents the window from being resized. If you want it to be resized, just set it as `TRUE`:

    ```
    glfwWindowHint(GLFW_RESIZABLE, GL_FALSE);
    ```

8. Next, we're going to create our window. For that, we'll add the following code:

    ```
    // Create a GLFWwindow object that we can use for GLFW's functions
    GLFWwindow *window = glfwCreateWindow(WIDTH, HEIGHT, "LearnOpenGL",
    nullptr, nullptr);
    ```

    In the preceding code, we call the values of the variables `WIDTH` and `HEIGHT`. These terms define the window's size and `"LearnOpenGL"` sets the title of our window. The window and the monitor variables are defined as null pointers and we'll deal with those in later chapters.

9. Next, we'll define variables for our screen's width and height because this will be the actual resolution that we want the window set to:

    ```
    int screenWidth, screenHeight;
    ```

Chapter 1

Then, in the following line of code with `glfwGetFramebufferSize`, we pass the references to the screen width and the screen height:

```
glfwGetFramebufferSize( window, &screenWidth, &screenHeight );
```

What this line of code actually does is it gets the actual width of the screen window itself, relative to the density of the screen. You could effectively omit these lines when you create an OpenGL viewport and just use `screenWidth` and `screenHeight` values only. But if you have something like a Mac or a Retina Mac, which is not natively 1920 x 1080, or, for example, a higher-density screen with a resolution like 3840 x 2160, the window would just get messed up. The content would be displayed in either the bottom-left of the screen or in the top-left. The previous line of code helps us in getting the actual width and height of our window, relative to any pixel density changes. So it's recommended to have it, as it will ensure maximum compatibility in the future, as more and more high resolution screens are coming out.

10. Now, we would want to check the window was created successfully, and we'll do that as follows:

```
if (nullptr == window)
{
    std::cout << "Failed to create GLFW window" << std::endl;
    glfwTerminate();

    return EXIT_FAILURE;
}
```

In the preceding code, we check the `nullptr == window` condition and we let the user know that something has gone wrong. Then, we just terminate anything that has been initialized with `glfwTerminate();`, and finally exit:

```
glfwMakeContextCurrent(window);
```

11. Next, we need to enable GLEW and we'll do that as follows:

```
// Set this to true so GLEW knows to use a modern approach to
retrieving function pointers and extensions
    glewExperimental = GL_TRUE;
```

Looking at `glewExperimental` in the code, you might wonder are we using experimental features? And, why have we to set it to `TRUE`? The reason for that is GLEW knows to use a modern approach to retrieve functions, pointers, and extensions. Basically, it's just a way of saying we're using GLEW the new and the modern way, but it's not necessarily an experimental function.

Setting Up OpenGL

12. Then, we're going to initialize GLEW and make sure it's successfully initialized in one go:

    ```
    // Initialize GLEW to setup the OpenGL Function pointers
    if (GLEW_OK != glewInit())
    {
            std::cout << "Failed to initialize GLEW" << std::endl;
            return EXIT_FAILURE;
    }
    ```

You can also use `return -1` instead of `return EXIT_FAILURE;` for Xcode.

13. Next, we'll set up the OpenGL viewport:

    ```
    // Define the viewport dimensions
    glViewport(0, 0, screenWidth, screenHeight);
    ```

    What we did in the preceding line of code is that we set the initial coordinates from 0, 0 to `screenWidth` and `screenHeight`. The values that you'll retrieve here will be an accurate representation of what our window is relative to the screen, as you might have a higher or a lower pixel density screen.

14. So now that we have set up the view port, we'll create our game loop:

    ```
    // Game loop
    while (!glfwWindowShouldClose(window))
    {
            // Check if any events have been activiated (key pressed,
            //mouse moved etc.) and call corresponding response functions
            glfwPollEvents();

            // Render
            // Clear the colorbuffer
            glClearColor(0.2f, 0.3f, 0.3f, 1.0f);
            glClear(GL_COLOR_BUFFER_BIT);

            // Draw OpenGL


            glfwSwapBuffers(window);
    }
    ```

Chapter 1

In the preceding code, we created a `While` loop and initialized it to check whether the window is open; if it is, then run the loop. In the loop, we are clearing `colorbuffer` with the help of the `glClearColor` function. `ClearColor` is actually an optional line of code, but the reason we are adding it is if we don't add this, we might just get a blank, black background because we haven't drawn anything yet. So instead of a black background, we tried to spruce it up with some color. We defined colors in a range between 0 and 1, which is quite similar to a range between 0 and 255, where 0 is of no value and 1 is the full intensity of red, green, blue, and alpha.

15. Then, we added `glClear` to clear our window so that we're ready to draw the next frame and put in `GL_COLOR_BUFFER_BIT;`. Here is where you would draw your OpenGL stuff. As we are not going to draw anything in this chapter, we'll add `glfwSwapBuffers` and provide it to the window. Then, we'll add `glfwTerminate` to close the window after the `while` loop is executed:

    ```
    // Terminate GLFW, clearing any resources allocated by GLFW.
    glfwTerminate();

    return EXIT_SUCCESS;
    }
    ```

> **TIP**: You can also use `return -1` instead of `return EXIT_FAILURE;` for Xcode.

Now, let's run this code and check the output. You will get a similar OpenGL window on your screen:

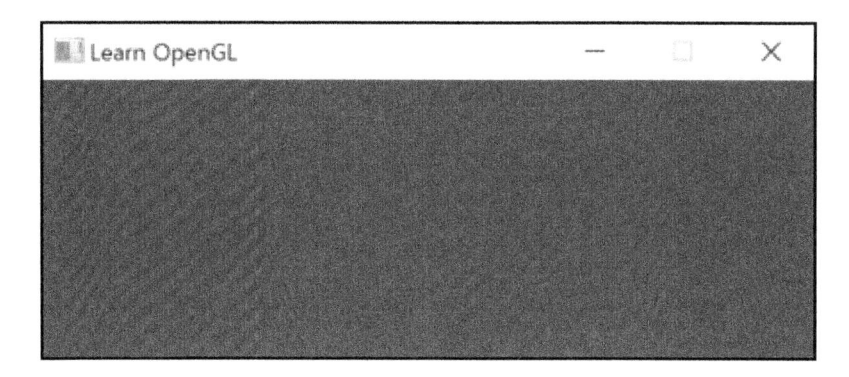

OpenGL rendering window for Windows

[29]

Setting up OpenGL using SDL on Windows

In this section, we'll discuss how to set up OpenGL on a Windows machine using SDL and GLEW. **SDL** stands for **Simple DirectMedia Layer**, and it allows us to create a render window and provides access to input devices through OpenGL. SDL is prominently used to code games and other media applications that run on various operating systems. It's a cross-platform multimedia library written in the C language. **GLEW (OpenGL Extension Wrangler)**, as seen in the previous sections, allows us to easily use extensions and non-core OpenGL functionality.

Downloading the SDL library

We'll begin the setup by downloading the essential libraries. Let's first download the SDL library by following these steps:

1. Visit `http://libsdl.org/index.php`, go to **Download**, and click on the latest version; at the time of writing this book, SDL 2.0 was the latest version.
2. Once you have clicked on the latest version, you may either want to download the development libraries or the runtime libraries. For this project, it is recommended that you download **Development Libraries**.
3. We'll go for the Visual C++ one, which is `SDL2-devel-2.0.8-VC.zip`. Click on the filename and download it.
4. Once you've downloaded the file, unzip it and put it in the `SDL` folder inside the `OpenGL` folder that we created in previous sections.
5. After downloading the SDL library, we move on to downloading the GLEW libraries, but as we've already downloaded them in the previous sections, you can just refer to that.

> If you want a quick review on downloading GLEW, you can refer to the *Downloading the essential libraries* section at the start of the chapter.

Setting up OpenGL using SDL and GLEW with absolute linking

Follow these steps to set up the environment in Visual Studio for OpenGL using SDL and GLEW with absolute linking:

1. Open up Visual Studio and click on **Create new Project...** in the home page window.
2. Go to **Visual C++** | **Windows Desktop** | **Windows Console Application**, name your project SDLOpenGL, and then click **OK.**
3. Next, right-click on the project in the **Solution Explorer** window. Click on **Properties.**
4. A **Property Pages** window will pop up, click on **C/C++** | **General**, and then go to **Additional Include Directories**. Click on the dropdown, then click on **Edit**, and you will get a pop up window.
5. Click on the **New** button, and then click on the three dots. And now, you want to go to SDL in the OpenGL folder. Select include and then click on the **Select Folder** button. Repeat the same process for including GLEW files. Once both the files have been included, click on the **OK** button.
6. Now, again in the **Property Pages** window, we'll go to **Linker** | **General**, and then go to **Additional Library Directories**. Click on the dropdown, then click on **Edit**, and you will get a pop-up window.
7. In the window, click on the **New** button, then click on the three dots, and go to the SDL folder. Open the lib folder, go to **x86** (which is a 32-bit file, actually), and then click on the **Select Folder** button.
8. Repeat the same process for including GLEW libraries. Open the lib folder, then double-click on the Release folder, select **Win32**, and then click on the **Select Folder** button. Once you have added both the libraries, click on the **OK** button.
9. Next, we'll go to **Linker** | **Input,** and then go to **Additional Dependencies.** Click on the dropdown, then click on **Edit**, and type opengl32.lib. Then, we'll type glew32s.lib. If you don't want to statically link the library, you can just remove the s. Next, we'll type SDL2.lib and SDL2main.lib, and then click on **OK**.
10. Then, click on the **Apply** button.

Setting up OpenGL using SDL and GLEW with relative linking

In this section, we'll take a look at how to set up OpenGL using SDL and GLEW as the provider for creating a render window with relative linking. Follow these steps:

1. Click on **Create new project...** and go to **Visual C++**. Select **Windows Console Application** and name it something like `SDLApp`.
2. Then, in the **New Project** window, click on the **Browse...** button. Go to the `OpenGL` folder that you created on the desktop and placed the downloaded libraries into `External Libraries`. Just select the folder and then click **OK**.
3. Now, we'll right-click on the project in the **Solution Explorer** window. Go to **Add | New Item**, and you will get an **Add New Item** window. Select **C++ File**, as this will be our main entry point; let's name it `main.cpp` and then click on the **Add** button.
4. Next, again right-click on the project in the **Solution Explorer** window. Click on **Properties.**
5. A **Property Pages** window will pop up. Click on **C/C++ | General** and then go to **Additional Include Directories**. Click on the dropdown, and then click on **Edit**.
6. Then, click on the **New** button and type `$(SolutionDir)` in the textbox. This command refers to the folder that contains our `.sln` file. So if we were to specify a folder in the path, and whenever we do something new in the project, it'd be relatively linked to wherever that file is located.

7. To link up the include files, add the paths, as shown in the following screenshot:

Additional Include Directories

$(SolutionDir)/../External Libraries/SDL/include
$(SolutionDir)/../External Libraries/GLEW/include

Evaluated value:

C:\Users\FrahaanAmanAziz\Desktop\OpenGL\GLApp\../External Libra
%(AdditionalIncludeDirectories)

Inherited values:

☑ Inherit from parent or project defaults

Setting Up OpenGL

8. Next, we'll link up the libraries. So, go to **Linker | General**, and then go to **Additional Library Directories**. Click on the dropdown and then click on **Edit**. Click on **New** and add the paths, as shown in the following screenshot, then click **OK**, and click **Apply**:

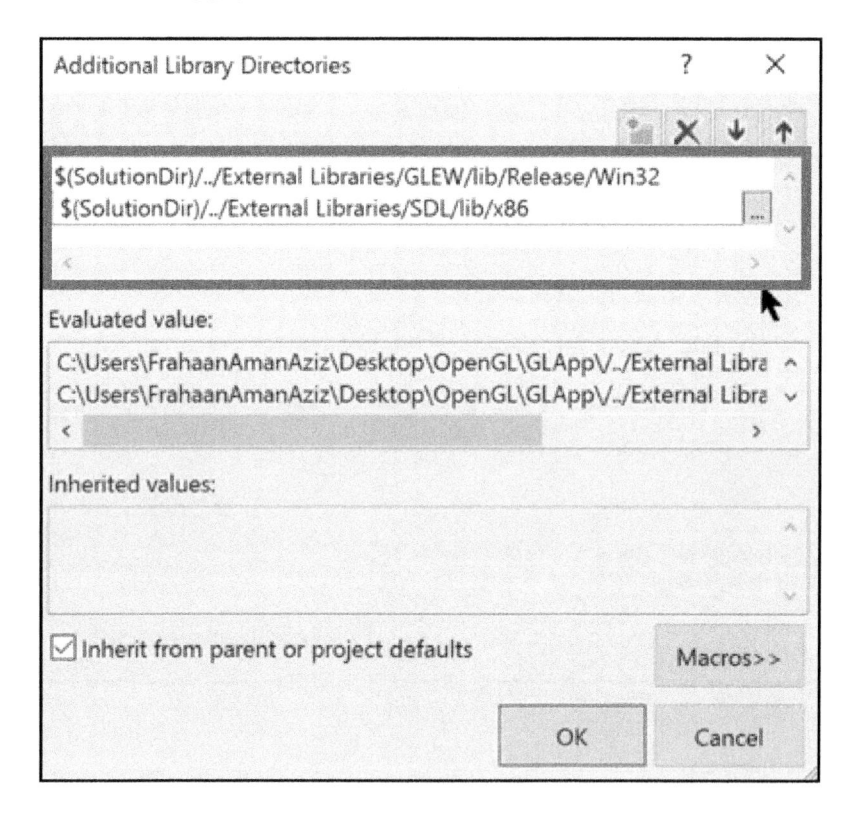

![Additional Library Directories dialog showing paths $(SolutionDir)/../External Libraries/GLEW/lib/Release/Win32 and $(SolutionDir)/../External Libraries/SDL/lib/x86]

9. Next, we'll link up the `.lib` files. So, go to the dropdown and click **Edit**. Now, just type in `opengl32.lib`. Then, we'll type `glew32s.lib`. Next, we'll type `SDL2.lib` and `SDL2main.lib`, and then click on **OK**.
10. Then, click on the **Apply** button.

Adding a DLL file to the project

As we saw in the previous sections, before completing the setup, we'll have to copy the dynamic link library into our project. Follow these steps to do that:

1. Go to `C:\OpenGL\SDL\lib\x86` and copy the `SDL2.dll` dynamic link library, as seen in the following screenshot:

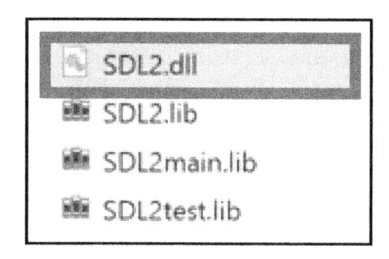

SDL2.dll dynamic link library

2. Now, go to the location in your system where the `main.cpp` file of your project is located and paste the dynamic link library there. We'll also have to copy and paste the `glew32.dll` file here from the `bin` folder of the `GLEW` folder.

Setting up OpenGL using SDL on a Mac

Here, we'll take a look at how to set up OpenGL using SDL on a Mac system. We'll begin by downloading the essential libraries on your system. As seen in the previous sections, we'll be using Homebrew to download the packages and libraries.

Downloading the SDL and GLEW libraries

In the Terminal, type the following command to download and install the SDL libraries:

```
brew install sdl2
```

Now, just press *Enter* and the SDL library will be downloaded onto your system. Next, we'll download the GLEW library, but since we've already downloaded it in the previous section, you can refer to that. If you want a quick review on downloading GLEW, you can refer to the *Downloading the GLFW and GLEW libraries for a Mac* section.

Setting Up OpenGL

Setting up Xcode for OpenGL using SDL

Follow these steps:

1. Open up Xcode and click on **Create a new Xcode project**.
2. Go to **OS X | Application**, then select **Command Line Tool**, and click **Next**.
3. You will get the following window. Fill in the necessary details, as highlighted in the screenshot, and make sure for the **Language** option, **C++** is selected:

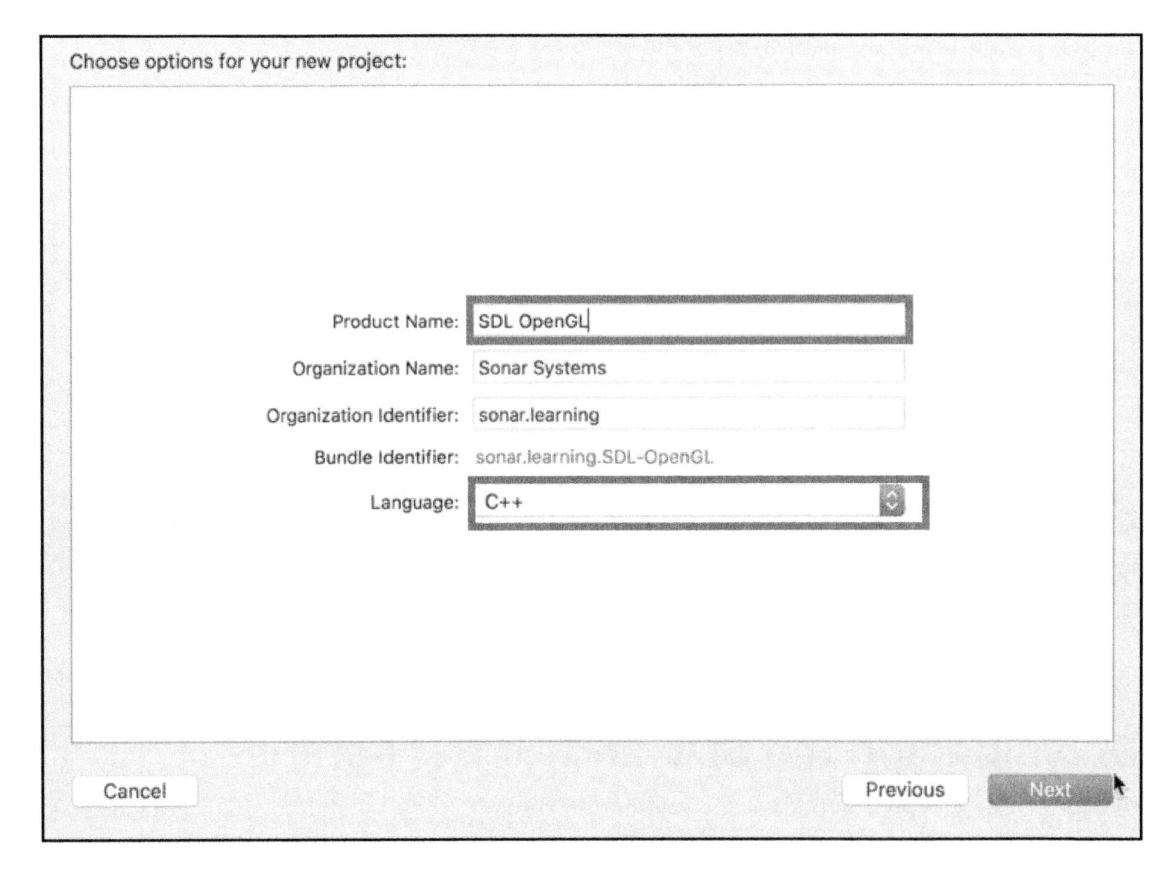

Details of the project

4. Then, set the location where you would like to store and save the project, and then click on the **Create** button.

5. Next, click on your project and go to **Build Settings**. In **Build Settings**, go to the **Search Paths** section and click on **Header Search Paths**. Then, click on **+** and type `/usr/local/include`. This will allow us to #include GLEW and SDL header files in our `main.cpp`.
6. Now go to **Build Phases**, then click on **Link Binary With Libraries**, and click the **+** button. Type `opengl` in the search bar, select `OpenGL.framework`, and then click on the **Add** button.
7. Again click on the **+** button, and then click on **Add Other....** Now, press *Cmd + Shift + G*, and it will open up a `go-to` folder search bar. In it, type `/usr/local`. Then click on **Cellar**, go to the **glew** | **lib** folder, select `libGLEW.1.12.0.dylib` without the little arrow, and click on **Open**.
8. Click **+** again, then click **Add Other....** Press *Cmd + Shift + G* and type `/usr/local`. Now go to **Cellar**, and go to **sdl** | **lib**. Select the non-alias `libSDL2-2.0.0.dylib` and click on the **Open** button.

With all the steps executed, our project is now set up to use SDL and GLEW with OpenGL on a Mac. We can now go to the `main.cpp` file and start writing our code for creating the OpenGL rendering window.

Creating the OpenGL rendering window using SDL

Perform the following steps to understand how to create a rendering window using SDL:

1. Let's go to our `main.cpp` file in Visual Studio or Xcode and let's get started. The first thing to do is include `iostream`; this'll be used to log out any errors that we have:

    ```
    #include <iostream>
    ```

2. Then, we'll include other necessary header files, such as the following:

    ```
    #include <SDL.h>

    #include <GL/glew.h>

    #include <SDL_opengl.h>
    ```

3. Next, we'll create a constant variable using `GLint`:

    ```
    const GLint WIDTH = 800, HEIGHT = 600;
    ```

Setting Up OpenGL

The reason for using `Glint` is quite simple: a regular `int` on different compilers might have different sizes, whereas `GLint` is always consistent. The `WIDTH` and the `HEIGHT` variables will store the size of our window.

4. Then, we'll set up our main entry point:

```
int main(int argc, char *argv[])
{
```

You might have noticed we have passed the `argc` integer and the `*argv []` as `char`. These are the argument count and the argument value and SDL requires them to run the code, or else you will get errors while running it.

5. Next, we'll initialize SDL with the help of `SDL_Init()` and to it we'll pass `SDL_INIT_EVERYTHING` to make sure we are initializing every part of the SDL library:

```
SDL_Init(SDL_INIT_EVERYTHING);
```

6. Then, we'll set up some attributes, which are essentially properties that we'll set for our window:

```
SDL_GL_SetAttribute(SDL_GL_CONTEXT_PROFILE_MASK,
SDL_GL_CONTEXT_PROFILE_CORE);
```

So, there are three main profiles that we can use for OpenGL with SDL:

- ES, which is embedded systems, for stuff like mobile devices
- There's the core profile, which is for modern OpenGL
- Then there's the compatibility profile, which allows you to use an older version of OpenGL and ensures maximum compatibility.

For our project, we'll use the core profile.

7. Next, we'll set up some more attributes, as follows:

```
SDL_GL_SetAttribute(SDL_GL_CONTEXT_MAJOR_VERSION, 3);
SDL_GL_SetAttribute(SDL_GL_CONTEXT_MINOR_VERSION, 3);
SDL_GL_SetAttribute(SDL_GL_STENCIL_SIZE, 8);
```

8. Once all the attributes have been declared, we'll declare the SDL window, as follows:

```
SDL_Window *window = SDL_CreateWindow("OpenGL", 0, 0, WIDTH,
HEIGHT, SDL_WINDOW_OPENGL);
```

The preceding code contains the name of our window, `OpenGL`. Then, we set the position of our window to `(0, 0)`. To set the width and the height of our window, we'll use the `WIDTH` and `HEIGHT` values that we declared earlier. The beauty of using these values is if we refer to these anywhere, they'll get updated if we were to change them later.

9. Next, for the context, we just need to provide the window variable that we created before:

    ```
    SDL_GLContext context = SDL_GL_CreateContext(window);

    // Set this to true so GLEW knows to use a modern approach to
    retrieving function pointers and extensions
    glewExperimental = GL_TRUE;
    ```

10. Now, we are going to initialize GLEW and ensure that it's has been initialized by checking for the condition in an `if` statement. If it hasn't been initialized, we're going to notify the user or the developer about it in the console:

    ```
    // Initialize GLEW to setup the OpenGL Function pointers
    if (GLEW_OK != glewInit())
    {
        std::cout << "Failed to initialize GLEW" << std::endl;
        return EXIT_FAILURE;
    }
    ```

11. Now, we'll set up the OpenGL viewport, as follows:

    ```
    // Define the viewport dimensions
    glViewport(0, 0, WIDTH, HEIGHT);
    ```

    What we did in the preceding line of code is that we set the initial coordinates from 0, 0 to `Width` and `Height`. The values that you'll retrieve here will be the accurate representation of what our window is relative to the screen, as you might have a higher or a lower pixel density screen. Next, we're going to create a window event, as follows:

    ```
    SDL_Event windowEvent;
    ```

12. Now, we'll create our game loop:

    ```
    while (true)
    {
        if (SDL_PollEvent(&windowEvent))
        {
            if (windowEvent.type == SDL_QUIT) break;
    ```

Setting Up OpenGL

```
            }

            // Clear the colorbuffer
            glClearColor(0.2f, 0.3f, 0.3f, 1.0f);
            glClear(GL_COLOR_BUFFER_BIT);

            // draw OpenGL

            SDL_GL_SwapWindow(window);
        }

        SDL_GL_DeleteContext(context);
        SDL_DestroyWindow(window);
        SDL_Quit();

        return EXIT_SUCCESS;
    }
```

In the preceding code, we set `while` to `true` to keep the loop constantly running while our application is open. If something happens, like the user closes the application, we'll exit the `while` loop and do some cleanup. While the loop is running, we'll check for a window event and pass a reference to the window. We'll also check if the window is getting shut down and if it is, then we'll break out of the loop. Now, outside of both the `if` statements, we'll try to clear the screen with the help of the `glClearColor` statement. A `ClearColor` statement isn't necessary. We're adding it because we might just end up getting a black background, as we're not drawing any shapes or any textures at the moment. We'll add color to the window with the help of the following parameters: `0.2f`, `0.3f`, `0.3f`, and `1.0f`. These values range between 0 and 1; these are very similar to 0 to 255. And these are red, green, blue, and alpha values. Next, we'll clear the screen with the help of `glClear`. And, the last thing we're going to do is `SDL_GL_SwapWindow`. It swaps the window if double buffering is present; if not, then it won't. Then, we'll do some cleanup and exit out of the code with `EXIT_SUCCESS`.

Now, let's run this code and check the output. You will get the same OpenGL window as we got in the preceding sections.

Setting up OpenGL using SFML on Windows

In this section, we'll study how to set up OpenGL using SFML and GLEW on a Windows machine. But, first, let's understand what SFML is. **SFML** is a simple and fast multimedia library. It's a software development library designed for cross-platform use to provide a programming interface for various multimedia components on the system. It allows you to do stuff like handle or render windows, so we can draw our OpenGL and handle events, such as various inputs, and it also allows us to handle textures.

Downloading the SFML library

Let's download the SFML library onto your system by visiting https://www.sfml-dev.org/index.php. Then, go to **Download**, click on **SFML 2.5.0**, and then select whichever Visual C++ version matches your Visual Studio version and system compatibility, and accordingly click on the link. The file will be downloaded as a ZIP file onto your system. Next, go to the OpenGL folder (which we created in the previous sections) and inside it, create a folder called SFML to extract and place our SFML files.

Linking the SFML and GLEW libraries to the project

The steps to link the SFML and GLEW libraries to our project with absolute or relative linking are similar to what we discussed in the previous sections. The only difference will be in the step where we link up the .lib files. For that, go to **Additional Dependencies** and in the textbox, just type in opengl32.lib. Then, we'll type glew32s.lib. And to link SFML libraries, we'll type sfml-graphics.lib, sfml-system.lib, and sfml-window.lib, and then click on **OK**.

Adding a DLL file to the project

As seen in the previous sections, before we begin with coding, we need to place the dynamic link library into our project. To do that, go to C:\OpenGL\SFML\bin\ and copy sfml-graphics-2.dll, sfml-system-2.dll, and sfml-window-2.dll, and paste them into the location in your system where the main.cpp file of your project is located. We'll also have to copy and paste the glew32.dll file here from the bin folder of the GLEW folder.

Setting Up OpenGL

With this, we are all set to code our OpenGL rendering window using SFML.

Setting up OpenGL using SFML on a Mac

The steps to download and link the SFML and GLEW libraries to our project will be similar to the previous sections where we discussed linking the GLFW and SDL libraries to the project on a Mac system.

With the setup process complete, let's move on to coding our OpenGL rendering window.

Creating the OpenGL rendering window using SFML

Check out the below mentioned steps:

1. Go to your `main.cpp` file in Visual Studio or Xcode and begin typing the following code:

   ```
   #include <iostream>
   ```

2. Here, we'll include the GLEW and SFML libraries in our project:

   ```
   #include <GL/glew.h>

   #include <SFML/Window.hpp>

   const GLint WIDTH = 800, HEIGHT = 600;
   ```

   In the preceding lines of code, we've defined the `GLint` constant. The reason we're creating constant global variables is so that we can easily use these wherever we need them in the code, whether that's for initially creating the window or for manipulating some sort of shape.

3. Next, let's define our entry point:

   ```
   int main( )
   {
      sf::ContextSettings settings;
      settings.depthBits = 24; settings.stencilBits = 8;
   ```

[42]

In the preceding lines of code, we've defined some settings for our application and rendering window:

```
settings.majorVersion = 3;
settings.minorVersion = 3;
settings.attributeFlags = sf::ContextSettings::Core;
```

Here, the `majorVersion` and `minorVersion` that we defined in the preceding lines of code are for setting the version of OpenGL. Here, we set the version as 3.3 by setting the `minorVersion` and the `majorVersion` to 3. If you wish to set up for any other version, you'll have to make changes accordingly. The `majorVersion` is to the left of the decimal point and the `minorVersion` is to the right of the decimal point. Then, we defined that we're using core modern OpenGL by setting `ContextSettings` to `Core`.

4. Next, you want to define `sf::Window`. Here, we're going to put `sf::VideoMode`, and we're going to put WIDTH, HEIGHT, and 32 for the pixel depth. Then, we'll add OpenGL SFML as the title of our window. And then, we add `sf::Style::Titlebar` and `sf::Style::Close` to have a title bar and a close button for our window:

```
sf::Window window( sf::VideoMode( WIDTH, HEIGHT, 32 ), "OpenGL
   SFML", sf::Style::Titlebar | sf::Style::Close, settings );
```

5. Now, we'll try to initialize GLEW by setting it to TRUE and if it's unsuccessful, then we'll display a `Failed to initialize GLEW` message to the developer. And then, we're going to do `return EXIT_FAILURE` because it has failed:

```
glewExperimental = GL_TRUE;

if ( GLEW_OK != glewInit( ) )
{
   std::cout << "Failed to initialize GLEW" << std::endl;

   return EXIT_FAILURE;
}

bool running = true;
```

6. Next, we are going to create a `while` loop and define certain conditions in it:

```
while ( running )
{
   sf::Event windowEvent;
```

Setting Up OpenGL

```
while ( window.pollEvent( windowEvent ) )
{
   switch ( windowEvent.type )
   {
   case sf::Event::Closed:
      running = false;

      break;
   }
}
```

In the preceding `while` loop, we are stating that if the window is closed, we are going to stop running our application and break out of our loop.

7. Then, we'll add some color to our window and define a space to draw:

```
    glClearColor( 0.2f, 0.3f, 0.3f, 1.0f );
    glClear( GL_COLOR_BUFFER_BIT );

    // draw OpenGL

    window.display( );
  }

  window.close( );

  return EXIT_SUCCESS;
 }
}
```

Let's run our code and check whether there are any errors. If no errors pop up, we'll get a rendering window as output, similar to what we have witnessed in the previous sections.

Summary

In this chapter, we discussed how to set up OpenGL using various libraries: GLFW, GLEW, SDL, and SFML. We learned how to set up our OpenGL projects on Windows and Mac. And, we also discussed how to link the libraries to our projects using absolute or relative linking. We then created rendering windows to display OpenGL graphics.

In the next chapter, we'll learn how to draw shapes like triangle and rectangle using OpenGL. Also, we'll discuss about how to apply colors and textures to the shapes.

Drawing Shapes and Applying Textures

2

The previous chapter was all about setting up our project to use different types of libraries, such as GLFW, GLEW, SMFL, and SDL. In this chapter, we'll go beyond the setup part and learn to implement some really cool OpenGL stuff. We'll learn about shaders and how to use them to create various shapes. Then, we'll move on to learn how to create a separate shader file and reference that in our code. We'll also discuss how to apply different textures to shapes using the SOIL library.

In this chapter, we'll cover the following topics in detail:

- Learning to draw a triangle using a shader
- Creating a separate shader file and referencing it in the main code
- Drawing a rectangle and applying textures to it using the SOIL library

This chapter will initiate you into OpenGL coding and you'll learn a lot of concepts related to it.

Before we get started with coding, there a few things that we need to understand. Firstly, the code we'll be writing from now on is platform- and framework-independent. So, it doesn't matter if you are using Xcode on Mac or Visual Studio on Windows, the OpenGL code on any platform will be the same, as OpenGL is a platform-independent programming language. Secondly, for this chapter, we'll be using the GLFW library. As we won't be writing any GLFW-specific code, the code in this chapter will be relevant for SFML, SDL, or any other library that you wish to use.

So, let's get started.

> You can refer to all the code files for this chapter in the `Chapter02` folder on GitHub. The GitHub link can be found in the preface of the book.

Drawing a triangle

In this section, we'll be looking at how to draw a triangle in OpenGL using the GLFW library. To begin with, let's go to the file in which we wrote code to create an OpenGL rendering window using the GLFW library in the previous chapter, and make the necessary changes to it. Let's take a look at the following steps to understand the code required to draw a triangle:

1. We'll begin by including the essential header files in our code:

    ```
    #include <iostream>
    // GLEW
    #define GLEW_STATIC
    #include <GL/glew.h>
    // GLFW
    #include <GLFW/glfw3.h>
    // Window dimensions
    const GLuint WIDTH = 800, HEIGHT = 600;
    ```

2. To create shapes in modern OpenGL, we need to create shaders. So, let's begin by adding some shaders to our code. Firstly, we'll add a constant, `GLchar *`, and we'll call it `vertexShaderSource`. This is going to be a string and its version will be `330 core`:

    ```
    // Shaders
    const GLchar* vertexShaderSource = "#version 330 core\n"
    ```

    The `330 core` defines the core shader language version for OpenGL version 3.3. If you're using OpenGL version 4.0, then the shader language version won't necessarily be `440`; it could be something different. By looking for it on the internet, you can get an idea of which shader version you should be using.

3. The `vertexShaderSource` that we mentioned in the preceding line of code is just going to handle the **location** and **positioning** of our triangle, which we'll define as follows:

    ```
    "layout (location = 0) in vec3 position;\n"
    "void main()\n"
    "{\n"
    "gl_Position = vec4(position.x, position.y, position.z, 1.0);\n"
    "}\0";
    ```

[46]

4. And in the following code, we'll have another shader source that is the `fragmentShaderSource`. This will handle the **color** and **texture** of our triangle. At the moment, we are explicitly setting only the color value in our shader, in the `vec4` variable:

   ```
   const GLchar* fragmentShaderSource = "#version 330 core\n"
   "out vec4 color;\n"
   "void main()\n"
   "{\n"
   "color = vec4(1.0f, 0.5f, 0.2f, 1.0f);\n"
   "}\n\0";
   ```

   To the variable `vec4` in the preceding code, we've assigned the values `1.0f`, `0.5f`, `0.2f`, and `1.0f`, which are the red, green, blue, and alpha values. The colors that we have defined here have ranges between 0 and 1, with 0 being off and 1 being full intensity; this is very similar to RGB color values ranging between 0 and 255.

5. Next, in the following lines of code, we will define our rendering window as discussed in the previous chapter, just take a look at the following code for review:

   ```
   // The MAIN function, from here we start the application and run the game loop
   int main()
   {
   // Init GLFW
   glfwInit( );

   // Set all the required options for GLFW
   glfwWindowHint( GLFW_CONTEXT_VERSION_MAJOR, 3 );
   glfwWindowHint( GLFW_CONTEXT_VERSION_MINOR, 3 );
   glfwWindowHint( GLFW_OPENGL_PROFILE, GLFW_OPENGL_CORE_PROFILE );
   glfwWindowHint( GLFW_OPENGL_FORWARD_COMPAT, GL_TRUE );

   glfwWindowHint( GLFW_RESIZABLE, GL_FALSE );

   // Create a GLFWwindow object that we can use for GLFW's functions
   GLFWwindow *window = glfwCreateWindow( WIDTH, HEIGHT, "LearnOpenGL", nullptr, nullptr );

   int screenWidth, screenHeight;
   glfwGetFramebufferSize( window, &screenWidth, &screenHeight );

   if ( nullptr == window )
   {
   ```

Drawing Shapes and Applying Textures

```
        std::cout << "Failed to create GLFW window" << std::endl;
        glfwTerminate( );

        return EXIT_FAILURE;
        }

        glfwMakeContextCurrent( window );
        // Set this to true so GLEW knows to use a modern approach to
        retrieving function pointers and extensions
        glewExperimental = GL_TRUE;
        // Initialize GLEW to setup the OpenGL Function pointers
        if ( GLEW_OK != glewInit( ) )
        {
        std::cout << "Failed to initialize GLEW" << std::endl;
        return EXIT_FAILURE;
        }

        // Define the viewport dimensions
        glViewport( 0, 0, screenWidth, screenHeight );
```

6. Now, before the `while` loop, we'll add a line of code to define our shader. Let's begin by adding the following code to our program:

```
        // Build and compile our shader program
        // Vertex shader
        GLuint vertexShader = glCreateShader( GL_VERTEX_SHADER );
        glShaderSource( vertexShader, 1, &vertexShaderSource, NULL );
```

In the preceding lines of code, we created a variable for `vertexShader` and defined the source of the shader with `glShaderSource()`. And for that function, we passed the parameters, number 1 as a reference to the `vertexShaderSource`, and for the final parameter, we passed `NULL` for now.

7. Next, we are going to compile the shader using `glCompileShader()`, and in there we'll pass `vertexShader`. Then, we're going to check for any compilation errors using `GLint success`. We'll display these compilation errors to the developers in the form of a log. Therefore, we define a `char` variable, `infoLog`, and it's going to be an array of 512 items:

   ```
   glCompileShader( vertexShader );
   // Check for compile time errors
   GLint success;
   GLchar infoLog[512];
   ```

8. Then, we'll add `glGetShaderiv()` function to our code. Which will return in params the values of parameter for our shader object. For that function, we'll pass the parameters like `vertexShader`, the status of compilation `GL_COMPILE_STATUS` and then pass `&success`:

   ```
   glGetShaderiv( vertexShader, GL_COMPILE_STATUS, &success );
   ```

9. Next, we'll check whether our shader has successfully compiled with the help of an `if` statement. If it hasn't been successfully compiled, a shader log will be generated and it will let the developer know about the compilation errors. To display the errors, we'll add `glGetShaderInfoLog()` function and in it, we'll pass the parameters as `vertexShader`, `512`, `NULL`, and `infoLog`, and then add `std::cout << "ERROR::SHADER::VERTEX::COMPILATION_FAILED\n"` and log out the `infoLog` so we can see it in more depth:

   ```
   if ( !success )
    {
    glGetShaderInfoLog( vertexShader, 512, NULL, infoLog );
    std::cout << "ERROR::SHADER::VERTEX::COMPILATION_FAILED\n" <<
    infoLog << std::endl;
    }
   ```

Drawing Shapes and Applying Textures

10. Now, we'll do the same for the fragment shader, take a look at the following highlighted lines of code, to understand the changes made for the fragment shader:

    ```cpp
    // Fragment shader
    GLuint fragmentShader = glCreateShader( GL_FRAGMENT_SHADER );
    glShaderSource( fragmentShader, 1, &fragmentShaderSource, NULL );
    glCompileShader( fragmentShader );

    // Check for compile time errors
    glGetShaderiv( fragmentShader, GL_COMPILE_STATUS, &success );

    if ( !success )
    {
      glGetShaderInfoLog( fragmentShader, 512, NULL, infoLog );
      std::cout << "ERROR::SHADER::FRAGMENT::COMPILATION_FAILED\n" << infoLog <<    std::endl;
    }
    ```

11. Then, we are going to link the shaders. For that, we'll create a variable called `shaderProgram` and reference it in `glCreateProgram();`. The `glCreateProgram()` creates an empty program object and returns a non-zero value by which it can be referenced. A **program object** is an object to which shader objects can be attached.

12. Then, we'll define `glAttachShader();` function to attach our shaders. In there we're going to pass the `shaderProgram`, which is the variable that we just created in the previous step. And then we'll pass the shaders that we're attaching to it. So, the first one we'll pass is `vertexShader` and then we'll attach the `fragmentShader`. Then, we'll define the function `glLinkProgram();`, and we'll link the `shaderProgram` to it. Take a look at the following code to understand the description:

    ```cpp
    // Link shaders
    GLuint shaderProgram = glCreateProgram( );
    glAttachShader( shaderProgram, vertexShader );
    glAttachShader( shaderProgram, fragmentShader );
    glLinkProgram( shaderProgram );
    ```

Chapter 2

13. The next thing we're going to do is check for any linking errors, always remember to check for any errors in your code. We'll check the error as follows:

    ```
    // Check for linking errors
    glGetProgramiv( shaderProgram, GL_LINK_STATUS, &success );

    if ( !success )
    {
    glGetProgramInfoLog( shaderProgram, 512, NULL, infoLog );
    std::cout << "ERROR::SHADER::PROGRAM::LINKING_FAILED\n" << infoLog << std::endl;
    }
    glDeleteShader( vertexShader );
    glDeleteShader( fragmentShader );
    ```

    In the preceding line of code, we defined `glGetProgramiv()`; and referenced our `shaderProgram` to it as we'll be checking whether there are any errors present in the code. Then, we'll check for the link status and assign its result to success. Next, we checked whether the linking of the shaders was successful. If the linking was not successful, we do essentially the same as we did in the previous lines of code; that is we'll generate the error log.

    We define `glGetProgramInfoLog ()`; function and in there we pass the parameters such as `shaderProgram`, because that's what we're checking in the errors for. Then we pass in `512` for the number of items and `NULL` array and the `infoLog`, because this is what we're going to assign any error logs to. Then we enter the error message that need to be displayed for the developer.

    So, now that we've checked for any errors while linking our shader program, we can actually delete the vertex and fragment shaders because we'll no longer be using them as they're part of our shader program now. So, we typed `glDeleteShader()`; function and reference the vertex and fragment shaders to it.

14. Next, what we're going to do is define the vertex data so that we can actually draw the triangle in terms of position:

    ```
    // Set up vertex data (and buffer(s)) and attribute pointers
    GLfloat vertices[] =
    {
        -0.5f, -0.5f, 0.0f, // Left
         0.5f, -0.5f, 0.0f, // Right
         0.0f,  0.5f, 0.0f  // Top
    };
    ```

Drawing Shapes and Applying Textures

> **TIP**
> In the preceding code, if you wanted draw a quadrilateral, you would have to define four vertices.

In the preceding lines of code, we began by defining a float array, `vertices[]`, and in it we defined our left, right, and the top coordinates.

> For the coordinates that we defined, in OpenGL by default if you don't explicitly set them, the values of your screen range between -1 and 1. So, that the value 0 is in the middle and 0.5 is 25% of the away from the middle, or 75% is the away from the left-hand side. In later sections, we will look at changing that system so it's actually using more of the screen.

15. Now that we've got the `vertices[]` array created, what we need to do is create the **vertex buffer object** (**VBO**) and the **vertex array object** (**VAO**). We'll begin by defining GLuint variables VBO, VAO. Then, we're going to generate the vertex array by simply typing `glGenVertexArrays();`, and in this function, we'll pass 1 and a reference to VAO. Next, we'll generate the buffers by defining the function `glGenBuffers();` and to that, we'll pass 1 and pass reference VBO to it.

    ```
    GLuint VBO, VAO;
    glGenVertexArrays( 1, &VAO );
    glGenBuffers( 1, &VBO );
    ```

16. Then, we'll bind the vertex array object and then bind and set the vertex buffers, so let's get on with that. We'll add `glBindVertexArray();` function and pass VAO to it. Then, we'll add `glBindBuffer();` function and pass GL_ARRAY_BUFFER and VBO to it. Next, we'll add `glBufferData();` function and pass GL_ARRAY_BUFFER and `size()`. As we'll be checking the size of our vertices in a dynamic way that is the reason we passed the function `size()` and to this function we'll pass in the vertices that we are drawing, and then finally we're going pass GL_STATIC_DRAW. So, this is just the buffer data that we'll be using to draw our good stuff:

    ```
    // Bind the Vertex Array Object first, then bind and set vertex
    buffer(s) and attribute pointer(s).
    glBindVertexArray( VAO );

    glBindBuffer( GL_ARRAY_BUFFER, VBO );
    glBufferData( GL_ARRAY_BUFFER, sizeof( vertices ), vertices,
    GL_STATIC_DRAW );
    ```

17. Next, we'll create the vertex pointer, so we'll add the function

`glVertexAttribPointer()` and to this function, we'll pass the parameters as highlighted in the following code. Then, we'll enable the vertex array by typing `glEnableVertexAttribArray()` function and we'll pass 0 to it.

```
glVertexAttribPointer( 0, 3, GL_FLOAT, GL_FALSE, 3 * sizeof( GLfloat ), ( GLvoid * ) 0 );
glEnableVertexAttribArray( 0 );
```

18. Then, we'll bind the buffer, adding `glBindBuffer()` function to our code. This is going to take two values: `GL_ARRAY_BUFFER` and `0`.
19. Then to the next line, we'll add `glBindVertexArray()` function and this is going to be `0`. As we are unbinding the vertex array object over here. It's always a good thing to unbind any buffers or arrays to prevent strange bugs. Take a look at the following code:

```
glBindBuffer( GL_ARRAY_BUFFER, 0 );
// Note that this is allowed, the call to glVertexAttribPointer
//registered VBO as the currently bound vertex buffer object so
//afterwards we can safely unbind

 glBindVertexArray( 0 );
// Unbind VAO (it's always a good thing to unbind any buffer/array
//to prevent strange bugs)
```

Adding code to draw the shape

The next thing we are going to do is add code to draw the triangle:

1. We are going to draw the shape within our while loop. We'll want to draw it after the `glClear()` function. So, once the screen's been cleared and before the screen buffers have been swapped, we'll add function `glUseProgram()`. This will indicate what shader program we're using, and for our project, it is `shaderProgram` that we have linked our vertex and fragment shaders to.

Drawing Shapes and Applying Textures

2. Then, we'll add `glBindVertexArray();` function and we bind the VAO to it.
3. Next, we'll want to call `glDrawArrays();` function as this will finally draw our triangle. In the first thing that we'll pass in the `glDrawArrays();` function is the mode, that is `GL_TRIANGLES` or `GL_QUAD` or `GL_LINE`. Depending on how many vertices you have and what sort of object or shape you're trying to achieve, this will vary—we'll be covering it in more depth later in this chapter. The second parameter that we'll pass to `glDrawArrays();` function is 0 and the final parameter that we pass is 3, as we've put how many vertices are there in our shape as it's a triangle.
4. Then, add `glBindVertexArray()` function and to it we pass 0. We are just unbinding it.
5. Now, there's literally one last thing to do: cleaning up. We'll de-allocate all the resources once we've finished using them. So, outside of the loop, add `glDeleteVertexArrays()` function and assign 1, &VAO and then add `glDeleteBuffers()` function to delete the buffers. Take a look at the following code to understand the preceding code description, also observe the highlighted terms in the code:

```
// Game loop
while ( !glfwWindowShouldClose( window ) )
{
// Check if any events have been activiated (key pressed, mouse moved //etc.) and call corresponding response functions

glfwPollEvents( );

// Render
// Clear the colorbuffer
glClearColor( 0.2f, 0.3f, 0.3f, 1.0f );
glClear( GL_COLOR_BUFFER_BIT );

// Draw our first triangle
glUseProgram( shaderProgram );
glBindVertexArray( VAO );
glDrawArrays( GL_TRIANGLES, 0, 3 );
glBindVertexArray( 0 );

// Swap the screen buffers
glfwSwapBuffers( window );
}

// Properly de-allocate all resources once they've outlived their purpose
glDeleteVertexArrays( 1, &VAO );
```

```
glDeleteBuffers( 1, &VBO );

// Terminate GLFW, clearing any resources allocated by GLFW.
glfwTerminate( );

return EXIT_SUCCESS;
}
```

Now we are ready to run our code. Once it gets complied without any errors, you will get the following triangle as the output:

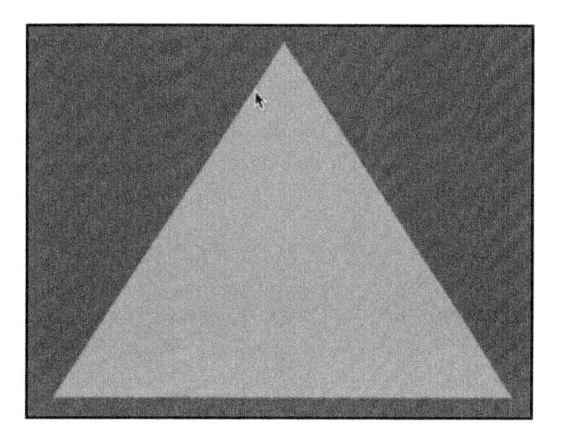

Abstracting the shaders

Let's take a look at shaders in this section, even though we've looked at shaders in the previous section while creating the triangle and using a shader to color it. What we're going to do in this section is to abstract the shader code into a vertex shader file and a fragment shader file so that it's a lot neater and more reusable. And, we're also going to abstract out the loading of the shader, as once we've abstracted that out, we probably won't need to change it at all, or at least there won't be too many changes to it. Further, in our projects, we'll just use these files to load the shaders in our code, which will make it easy to use.

Drawing Shapes and Applying Textures

Creating the shader files

Follow these steps to create the files:

1. We'll begin by creating two new empty files in our project IDE and name those two files `core.vs` and `core.frag`. Here, `vs` stands for vector shader file and `frag` stands for fragment shader file.

   > **TIP**: It doesn't actually matter what you name these as long as you refer to the exact name and the extension when you refer to them.

2. Then, open your `core.vs` file and cut and paste the `VectorShaderSource` code that we had added in the previous section. Make the highlighted changes shown in the following code:

   ```
   #version 330 core
   layout (location = 0) in vec3 position;
   layout (location = 1) in vec3 color;
   out vec3 ourColor;
   void main()
   {
     gl_Position = vec4(position, 1.0f);
     ourColor = color;
   }
   ```

   Let's save this file and our vector shader file is created. Next, we're going to do essentially the same for the fragment shader file.

3. So, let's open up `core.frag` in our IDE and cut and paste `fragmentShaderSource` code from the code in the previous section. Once pasted, make changes to it as highlighted in the following code:

   ```
   #version 330 core
   in vec3 ourColor;
   out vec4 color;
   void main()
   {
     color = vec4(ourColor, 1.0f);
   }
   ```

Save this file and we've now created the fragment shader file too. Let's move on to create the Shader.h file for abstracting the loading of shader code.

Creating the Shader.h header file

Now, we'll also create the shader loading file that is Shader.h and use that to load our shader into the code. Follow these steps to create the Shader.h file:

1. So, let's create an empty header file in our project and name that file Shader.h.
2. Once this file is created, open it and cut and paste the shader loading code from the code that we had mentioned in the previous section.
3. What we're actually going to do is cut everything just after the glViewport(0, 0, screenWidth, screenHeight); code and above the vertices array GLfloat vertices[] code. As the code that we cut was actually loading our shaders.
4. Then, make the changes shown in the following code:

   ```
   #ifndef SHADER_H
   #define SHADER_H
   #include <string>
   #include <fstream>
   #include <sstream>
   #include <iostream>
   #include <GL/glew.h>
   ```

   So, what we've got in the preceding lines of code is just some simple #ifndef and #define preventing it from being included multiple times. We're just including the stream and string headers because they're what we're going to be loading our files into, so we need the correct headers to load it. Then, we need GLEW obviously, which assumes you've got GLEW set up.

5. After that, we've got the GLuint program, and we've got some comments right there. We'll construct the shader on the fly:

   ```
   class Shader
   {
   public:
   GLuint Program;
   // Constructor generates the shader on the fly
   Shader( const GLchar *vertexPath, const GLchar *fragmentPath )
   {
   ```

Drawing Shapes and Applying Textures

6. The following variables are used to store and load the code and the shader file:

    ```
    // 1. Retrieve the vertex/fragment source code from filePath
    std::string vertexCode;
    std::string fragmentCode;
    std::ifstream vShaderFile;
    std::ifstream fShaderFile;
    ```

7. In the following code, we're just handling some exceptions:

    ```
    // ensures ifstream objects can throw exceptions:
    vShaderFile.exceptions ( std::ifstream::badbit );
    fShaderFile.exceptions ( std::ifstream::badbit );
    ```

8. In the following code we are using the string stream, what we're going to do is open the file so we've got the vertex and the fragment path. Using the string streams, we're reading the file into the actual stream itself. And then, because we don't need it anymore, we can just close it. Then, we'll load it into our strings and catch any errors there. It's very simple stuff if you've done C++ before, which we recommend you should be familiar with:

    ```
    try
    {
        // Open files
        vShaderFile.open( vertexPath );
        fShaderFile.open( fragmentPath );
        std::stringstream vShaderStream, fShaderStream;
        // Read file's buffer contents into streams
        vShaderStream << vShaderFile.rdbuf( );
        fShaderStream << fShaderFile.rdbuf( );
        // close file handlers
        vShaderFile.close( );
        fShaderFile.close( );
        // Convert stream into string
        vertexCode = vShaderStream.str( );
        fragmentCode = fShaderStream.str( );
    }

    catch ( std::ifstream::failure e )
    {
        std::cout << "ERROR::SHADER::FILE_NOT_SUCCESFULLY_READ" << std::endl;
    }
    ```

Chapter 2

9. After that, we're just getting the C string. Then, we're just compiling the shaders, which we've already done. So, after those first two lines of code, we're sort of done:

```
const GLchar *vShaderCode = vertexCode.c_str( );
const GLchar *fShaderCode = fragmentCode.c_str( );

// Compile shaders

GLuint vertex, fragment;
GLint success;
GLchar infoLog[512];

// Vertex Shader
vertex = glCreateShader( GL_VERTEX_SHADER );
glShaderSource( vertex, 1, &vShaderCode, NULL );
glCompileShader( vertex );
// Print compile errors if any
glGetShaderiv( vertex, GL_COMPILE_STATUS, &success );
if ( !success )
{
glGetShaderInfoLog( vertex, 512, NULL, infoLog );
std::cout << "ERROR::SHADER::VERTEX::COMPILATION_FAILED\n" << infoLog << std::endl;
}

// Fragment Shader
fragment = glCreateShader( GL_FRAGMENT_SHADER );
glShaderSource( fragment, 1, &fShaderCode, NULL );
glCompileShader( fragment );
// Print compile errors if any
glGetShaderiv( fragment, GL_COMPILE_STATUS, &success );
if ( !success )
{
    glGetShaderInfoLog( fragment, 512, NULL, infoLog );
    std::cout << "ERROR::SHADER::FRAGMENT::COMPILATION_FAILED\n" << infoLog << std::endl;
}

// Shader Program
this->Program = glCreateProgram( );
glAttachShader( this->Program, vertex );
glAttachShader( this->Program, fragment );
glLinkProgram( this->Program );
// Print linking errors if any
glGetProgramiv( this->Program, GL_LINK_STATUS, &success );
if (!success)
{
```

Drawing Shapes and Applying Textures

```
            glGetProgramInfoLog( this->Program, 512, NULL, infoLog );
            std::cout << "ERROR::SHADER::PROGRAM::LINKING_FAILED\n" <<
    infoLog << std::endl;
     }

    // Delete the shaders as they're linked into our program now and no
    //longer necessery
     glDeleteShader( vertex );
     glDeleteShader( fragment );

    }
```

10. And then here's a lower line, just saying to use the program:

    ```
    // Uses the current shader
     void Use( )
     {
     glUseProgram( this->Program );
     }
     };
    #endif
    ```

So, what we've done in the preceding code is make our shader code a bit more dynamic. Next, we're going to go to our `main.cpp` and carry out some changes to it.

Making changes to the draw triangle code

As we created our shader files and the `Shader.h` header file in the preceding sections, we'll now load those files into our triangle code. To do this, we'll have to make certain changes to the triangle code that we wrote earlier. Check out the below mentioned steps:

1. We'll begin by including the `Shader.h` header file, because without that we can't actually use the `Shader` class:

    ```
    #include "Shader.h"
    ```

2. Then, before defining our vertices, we'll add the following line of highlighted code:

    ```
    // Build and compile our shader program
     Shader ourShader( "core.vs", "core.frag" );
    ```

Chapter 2

For Xcode, this highlighted code will be replaced with the following line of code:
`Shader ourShader( "resources/shaders/core.vs", "resources/shaders/core.frag" );`
If you execute our triangle code without adding this line on Mac you will get an error and the triangle won't be generated in your output window. The reason this happens is there are executable files in your project folder, but we don't have any resource files. So, we'll have to add those file to our project:

> 1. What we want to do is go to our project folder in Xcode, right-click on it, go to **New Folder**, and create a folder called `resources`.
> 2. Inside the `resources` folder, we'll create another folder called `shaders`. And then in there, we create a folder that's called `images/videos` whenever we need those particular file types. So, this is going to be good for the future as well.
> 3. Next, what we'll do is move our shader files, `core.vs` and `core.frag`, into the `shader` folder.
> 4. Then, go to your project, go to **Build Phases**, and then click on **+** and click on the **New Copy Files Phase** option.
> 5. Once you've clicked that, you'll have a new section, **Copy Files (0 items)**. Open that and make sure **Destination** is set to **Resources**, and then click on the + sign below it.
> 6. Then, select the `resources` folder and click on the **Add** button.

3. Furthermore, there are a few changes that we want to make to our `vertices []` array. As you may remember when we created `core.vs`, what we did was we actually created an input for the color as well. So, instead of just explicitly setting the color, we're going to allow some sort of color input. And to do that, we're going to expand out the vertices array as follows:

```
GLfloat vertices[] =
{
    // Positions          // Colors
    0.5f, -0.5f, 0.0f,    1.0f, 0.0f, 0.0f,   // Bottom Right
    -0.5f, -0.5f, 0.0f,   0.0f, 1.0f, 0.0f,   // Bottom Left
    0.0f, 0.5f, 0.0f,     0.0f, 0.0f, 1.0f    // Top
};
```

Drawing Shapes and Applying Textures

In the preceding lines of code, what we actually did was added the color by putting the values for red, green, and blue color. This is going to be really exciting because we're assigning a color to each of the vertices, and what's going to happen is, it will blend the colors together and this will create a really amazing effect on our triangle.

4. Next, we'll go to our position attribute and color attribute code, and replace those with the following code:

```
// Position attribute
  glVertexAttribPointer( 0, 3, GL_FLOAT, GL_FALSE, 6 * sizeof( GLfloat ), ( GLvoid * ) 0 );
  glEnableVertexAttribArray( 0 );
// Color attribute
  glVertexAttribPointer( 1, 3, GL_FLOAT, GL_FALSE, 6 * sizeof( GLfloat ), ( GLvoid * )( 3 * sizeof( GLfloat ) ) );
  glEnableVertexAttribArray( 1 );
```

The preceding lines of code will define the position and color attributes of the triangle. In the `vertices []` as we've six values now: 3 for position coordinates and other 3 for color coordinates. That is the reason why we've put 6 in the preceding code because we've got 6 so we've got two values for each vertex and we've added color, so we need to add 6 to our code.

5. Next, we'll get rid of:

```
glBindBuffer( GL_ARRAY_BUFFER, 0 );
```

6. We'll then move on to our while loop and replace the `glUseProgram( shaderProgram )` with the following code:

```
ourShader.Use( );
```

With this preceding last minor change to our code, we are now ready to run our program. Once it's successfully complied without any errors, you will get the following colorful triangle as output on your screen:

Chapter 2

As we've added a color to each one of the vertices in the code. The color in the output triangle has blended together. That's what OpenGL does: it blends the colors together. Chances are if you've Googled OpenGL before, or just in general if you're into game development, you would have come across some sort of similar triangle like this. This is almost a rite of passage in OpenGL equivalent to the Hello World code in other programming languages.

Loading and applying textures to the shape

In this section, we'll look how to load textures in our code and learn to apply these textures to our objects. Textures is an image which is used add detail to an object. Imagine object such as cube and if we apply wooden texture to it, then it will look like a wooden box in our game world.

For this section, our object will be a rectangle. So first we'll learn how to draw rectangle shape in OpenGL and then understand how to apply textures to it. To apply texture to the shape, we'll prefer when using SOIL library, which is the Simple OpenGL Image Library. If you wish, you can use other libraries such as libpng which, as the name suggests, just supports PNG format images. But in this section, we'll only learn about SOIL, actually about SOIL2.

SOIL is a cross-platform library and it's supported on Android and iOS as part of game development. GLFW doesn't have any image loading methods built in, that is the reason why we are going to use SOIL library to load our textures. Also, SOIL helps in making our code as dynamic as possible across various platforms, and it's really easy to use as well.

[63]

Drawing Shapes and Applying Textures

So, first let's understand how to set up our project to use the SOIL library on Windows and Mac platform.

Setting up a project to use SOIL on Windows

In this section, we'll understand how to set up our project to use the SOIL library on a Windows platform. So, we'll begin by downloading the SOIL library and Premake. You must be wondering, what is Premake? Premake is a command line tool used to generate project files for platforms such as Visual Studio, Xcode, and so on.

Follow these steps to understand the set up process:

1. Open up your web browser and go to the following link `https://bitbucket.org/SpartanJ`. In the **Repositories** section click on the SOIL2 option and open the webpage, and select the first fork under **Introduction** for the latest version of SOIL library.

> **TIP:** The reason we are downloading the SOIL2 library is beacuse the original SOIL library is actually very old and hasn't been updated for a very long time.

2. Once you've downloaded that, just search for Premake on Google or visit the following link: `https://premake.github.io/`. Then, click on the **Download** option. It is recommended that you download the latest stable branch, so download the 4.4 version, which is currently stable (at the time of writing this book).
3. Next, go to the location where you've downloaded the files and extract both of the zipped folders.
4. Then, go to the `Premake` folder and copy and paste `premake4.exe` into the `SOIL` folder, which we just extracted.
5. Open up the command prompt and in here you may want to change the directory path to the location where you downloaded and extracted your `SOIL` folder. Suppose the `C:` drive is the drive where all your files get downloaded and you have downloaded and extracted your `SOIL` folder to that drive, then all you have to do is type `cd` in command prompt and then just drag and drop your `SOIL` folder into it. It will automatically enter the path where the `SOIL` folder is located.

> If it's any other drive that your downloads go to, then what you have to do is first tell command prompt to change it to that particular drive. To do that, just type the actual letter of the drive then type : and hit *Enter*, and then you can follow the previous drag-and-drop process.

6. Next, in Command Prompt, type in `premake4.exe`—or whatever the executable is called—followed by `vs2017` and then hit *Enter*. This will generate our Visual Studio project.

> If you're using an older version, such as 2010, you can use 2010 in the `vs` command. It doesn't have a command for newer versions of Visual Studio, but if you enter that, it will prompt you to upgrade some of the properties, so don't worry about that.

7. Now let's go to our `SOIL` folder, open the `make` folder present inside it and then open up the `Windows` folder.
8. Inside the `Windows` folder, you'll get a `SOIL2.sln` file. Double-click on it and once that has opened in Visual Studio, you might get an upgrade the compiler, and libraries pop window. Just click on the **OK** button.
9. Then, in the Visual Studio, on the right-hand side, you'll see a filenames. The only one that we're concerned with is `soil2-static-lib`. Right-click on that file and then click on **Build** option. This will build our project. You can then close Visual Studio.
10. Now, if you go back to the `SOIL` folder, there'll be some more folders generated. The one we're interested in is the `lib` folder.
11. Inside the `lib` folder, there's a `Windows` folder which consists of the `.lib` file, which is what we need.
12. Copy that `.lib` file and go to the location where you have your OpenGL project created. What we'll do there is, the location where `.sln` file is present, we'll make a new folder and name it as `External Libraries`.
13. In the `External Libraries` folder we will create a sub folder called `SOIL2`, and inside that, we'll create a folder called `lib`.

Drawing Shapes and Applying Textures

14. Then, in the `lib` folder that we created just now, paste the `soil2-debug.lib` file. So, this way we're going to use relative linking to link our SOIL library. If you are aware of the absolute linking process and wants to use it, you can use that.
15. And now, what we need to do is go back to the `SOIL` folder and copy the files present within the `SOIL2` folder and paste that in the `OpenGL_VisualStudio` folder which is present inside the `OpenGL` folder
16. So, once you've got all of these steps sorted, the one last thing to do is link up the `soil2-debug.lib` to our project. To link up the `.lib` file to our Visual Studio project with the relative linking, you can refer to the *Linking of GLFW and GLEW libraries with relative linking* section in the previous chapter.

With this, we have set up our project to use the SOIL library on Visual Studio.

Setting up a project to use SOIL on Mac

In this section, we'll understand how to set up our project to use the SOIL library on a Mac platform. Let's take a look at the following steps:

1. Open up your web browser and go to the following link: https://bitbucket.org/SpartanJ.
2. In the **Repositories** section click on the SOIL2 option and open the webpage, and select the first fork under **Introduction** for the latest version of SOIL library.
3. Next, go to the location where you've downloaded the files and extract them. Once extracted, go to the `src` folder and in it go to the `SOIL2` folder. Then just copy and paste that folder into your project directory in your system, which also contains your `main.cpp` and `shader` file.
4. Now, just add the library to our triangle project as you normally would. So, what we will do is right-click on the project in Xcode, go to the **Add Files** option, click on **SOIL**, and then click on the **Add** button.

So, once we've got that included, that's it for the setup part. And now, we'll go back to our the code from the previous section and make modification to it so as to add textures to our shape.

Applying texture to our shape

Now that we're all set up to use the SOIL library, let's go to our triangle code and make the necessary changes to load our shape and apply texture to it. Follow these steps:

1. So, we'll first include the SOIL library into our code; for that, type in the following line at the start of your code:

    ```
    #include SOIL2/SOIL2.h
    ```

    Here, we have typed `SOIL2/SOIL2.h` because our library is inside the `SOIL2` folder.

2. The next thing we're going to do is enable the alpha support for images with extension such as PNG. To do that, type in the following lines of code after we have defined out `glViewport()` :

    ```
    // enable alpha support
      glEnable( GL_BLEND );
      glBlendFunc( GL_SRC_ALPHA, GL_ONE_MINUS_SRC_ALPHA );
    ```

    In the preceding lines of code, the `glEnable( GL_BLEND )` function will help in blending the image in our shape. Then we used `glBlendFunc()` and to it we passed two parameters `GL_SRC_ALPHA` and `GL_ONE_MINUS_SRC_ALPHA`. This is how we enabled the alpha support.

3. Next, we'll have to modify our vertices as we'll be using a rectangular shape to apply our texture, and also we'll have to add coordinates for our texture too. So take a look at the following vertices array and make the necessary changes to your code:

    ```
    // Set up vertex data (and buffer(s)) and attribute pointers
      GLfloat vertices[] =
      {
      // Positions          // Colors            // Texture Coords
       0.5f,  0.5f, 0.0f,   1.0f, 0.0f, 0.0f,    1.0f, 1.0f, // Top Right
       0.5f, -0.5f, 0.0f,   0.0f, 1.0f, 0.0f,    1.0f, 0.0f, // Bottom Right
      -0.5f, -0.5f, 0.0f,   0.0f, 0.0f, 1.0f,    0.0f, 0.0f, // Bottom Left
      -0.5f,  0.5f, 0.0f,   1.0f, 1.0f, 0.0f,    0.0f, 1.0f  // Top Left
       };
    ```

Drawing Shapes and Applying Textures

As we're going to draw a rectangle, we need four different vertices: bottom left, bottom right, top left, and top right. In the preceding code, the values that we've added don't actually range between -1 and 1; these values range between 0 and 1 so are know as normalized values. You might hear this term in computer graphics quite a lot. Normalized values basically means the values ranged between 0 and 1. So, for example, if you had an image that has a width of 1280 x 1280, and the normalized version was 0 to 1, if you were to set a value of 0.5, it would be at 640 because it's halfway along and halfway between 0 and 1280 is 640. This is just a very basic overview of normalization. If you want to know a bit more about it, feel free to Google it.

4. The next thing we're going to create is another array for indices. Take a look at the following code and let's try to understand it:

```
GLuint indices[] =
{ // Note that we start from 0!
0, 1, 3, // First Triangle
1, 2, 3 // Second Triangle
};
```

The reason we've defined two triangles in the preceding array is, as we're drawing a quadrilateral in this section, our rectangle shape actually requires two triangle indices to be defined. Take a look at the following image to understand the concept:

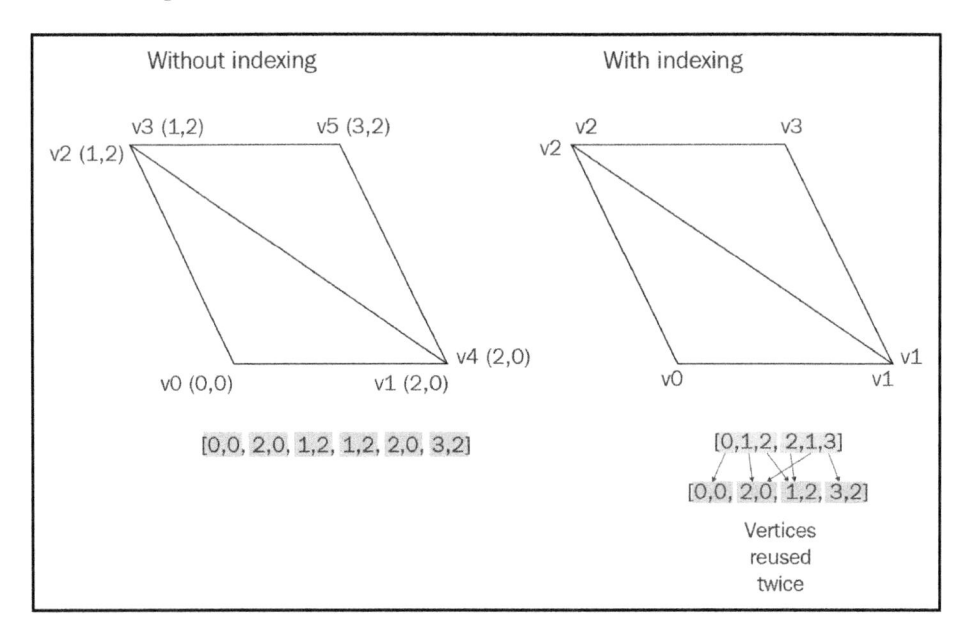

[68]

The preceding image shows defining of the triangle coordinates with and without indexing. So, let's have a look at the without indexing part. Without indexing, to draw a quadrilateral you'll need six different vertices, as seen in the image. Even though there are two pairs of similar coordinates that are shared between the two triangles, the vertices are not being efficiently defined. With indexing approach, however, we can share the vertices. So, as in the **with indexing** image, the two triangles share the same pair of vertices. So we'll reuse those and as a result, we'll be defining only four vertices. Ignore the numbering shown in the image; it's slightly different to our situation, but the principle still applies. And if you try and draw it out on paper and apply the numbers that we got in our indices array to the actual triangle or quadrilateral from the two, it will make a lot more sense. It might not be obvious why you would want to do this at the moment, and that's because we're only drawing a quadrilateral. But, imagine when you have a game and you've got thousands if not millions of triangles, and triangles forming various complex shapes. Thus this with indexing approach really becomes handy and increase the efficiency of your code.

5. Next, in our `GLuint` section below our indices, we want to create another buffer called `EBO`, so make the change to the code as highlighted in the following line:

    ```
    GLuint VBO, VAO, EBO;
    ```

6. We need to generate the buffers for the Element Buffer Objects (EBO), so type in the following highlighted lines of code and then we also need to bind that buffer :

    ```
    glGenVertexArrays(1,&VAO);
    glGenBuffers(1,&VBO );
    //Generating EBO
    glGenBuffers(1,&EBO );

    glBindVertexArray( VAO );

    glBindBuffer( GL_ARRAY_BUFFER, VBO );
    glBufferData( GL_ARRAY_BUFFER, sizeof( vertices ), vertices, GL_STATIC_DRAW );
    //Binding the EBO
    glBindBuffer( GL_ELEMENT_ARRAY_BUFFER, EBO );
    glBufferData( GL_ELEMENT_ARRAY_BUFFER, sizeof( indices ), indices, GL_STATIC_DRAW );
    ```

Drawing Shapes and Applying Textures

7. Next, we'll modify our position and the color attributes, and we'll add one more attribute that is the texture coordinate attribute. Let's check out the following highlighted code and try to understand the modifications done to it:

    ```
    // Position attribute
    glVertexAttribPointer( 0, 3, GL_FLOAT, GL_FALSE, 8 * sizeof(
    GLfloat ), ( GLvoid * ) 0 );
    glEnableVertexAttribArray(0);
    // Color attribute
    glVertexAttribPointer( 1, 3, GL_FLOAT, GL_FALSE, 8 * sizeof(
    GLfloat ), ( GLvoid * )( 3 * sizeof( GLfloat ) ) );
    glEnableVertexAttribArray(1);
    // Texture Coordinate attribute
    glVertexAttribPointer( 2, 2, GL_FLOAT, GL_FALSE, 8 * sizeof(
    GLfloat ), ( GLvoid * )( 6 * sizeof( GLfloat ) ) );
    glEnableVertexAttribArray( 2 );
    ```

    For the position and the color attributes in the preceding code, we have replaced 6 with 8, as we have eight coordinates in our vertices array: three for the position, three for the colors, and two for the texture coordinates. And then, we created another vertex attribute pointer as the texture coordinate attribute.

8. Next, we're going to add the texture loading code. In our main code, after we've unbinded our vertex array and before the start of `while` loop, we'll add the texture loading code.
9. Firstly we'll need to create an `GLuint texture` variable as this will hold our reference to the texture.
10. Next, we'll create `int` variables as `width` and `height`. This will define the width and the height of our texture.
11. Then we'll need to add `glGenTextures()` function and for this, we specify the `size` as `1` and put a reference to our texture variable.
12. We'll then bind the texture using `glBindTexture()` funtion. Take a look at the following highlighted code:

    ```
    glBindVertexArray( 0 ); // Unbind VAO

    // Load and create a texture
    GLuint texture;
    int width, height;
    // Texture
    glGenTextures( 1, &texture );
    glBindTexture( GL_TEXTURE_2D, texture );
    ```

13. And then, we are going to set our texture parameters. For that, we're going to add function `glTexParameteri ()` and to this function, we'll pass the following parameter:
    - The first parameter that we're going to set is `GL_TEXTURE_2D`
    - Then for the `name` we're going to set the type of wrapping that we'll be using `GL_TEXTURE_WRAP_S`.
    - And for the wrapping, we're going to add `GL_REPEAT`.

> It is recommended you have a look at different wrapping techniques. You can find more information about this in the OpenGL API guides and if you look at `learnopengl.com` and `open.gl`, you will get to read a lot more information about all the lines of code that we have written.

14. So, what we're going to do next is duplicate the previous line of code and make the following changes as highlighted in the code:

    ```
    // Set our texture parameters
    glTexParameteri( GL_TEXTURE_2D, GL_TEXTURE_WRAP_S, GL_REPEAT );
    glTexParameteri( GL_TEXTURE_2D, GL_TEXTURE_WRAP_T, GL_REPEAT );
    ```

15. Next, we're going to set the texture filtering. Check out the following code for it:

    ```
    // Set texture filtering
    glTexParameteri( GL_TEXTURE_2D, GL_TEXTURE_MIN_FILTER, GL_LINEAR );
    glTexParameteri( GL_TEXTURE_2D, GL_TEXTURE_MAG_FILTER, GL_LINEAR );
    ```

16. Now, we are going to add the actual texture loading code to the main code. For that, we're going to create unsigned char variable `*image` and this will hold the reference to the function `SOIL_load_image()`. And to this function we pass the following parameters:
    - First parameter will be the path of the actual image that we're going to use as texture for our object. Therefore, we'll put `res/images/image1.jpg`.
    - The second parameter will be the refrence to the width and the height of our image.

Drawing Shapes and Applying Textures

- Then for the third parameter, we're just going to pass it as 0.
- For the fourth parameter we're going to set the loading method so will add `SOIL_LOAD_RGBA`. Even if it's a JPEG image, you always want to load it as an alpha image. The reason for that is, it allows the code that we're writing now to be more dynamic. So if we swap the JPEG image for a PNG image, it'll still work. If you put in a different type of alpha image, or an image without alpha, as long as that type is supported by SOIL, the code will work fine.

```
unsigned char *image = SOIL_load_image(
"res/images/image1.jpg", &width, &height, 0, SOIL_LOAD_RGBA );
```

17. Next, we'll specify a two-dimensional texture image adding the function `glTexImage2d()` and to this function we are going to pass the highlighted parameters in the following code:

```
// Load, create texture
glTexImage2D( GL_TEXTURE_2D, 0, GL_RGBA, width, height, 0, GL_RGBA,
GL_UNSIGNED_BYTE, image );
```

18. We'll generate the mipmaps, so we're going to put `glGenerateMipmap()` funtion. And for this function, we specify `GL_TEXTURE_2D` as it's a 2D texture that we are using.
19. Then, we're going to free our image data, as it's always good to clean up. So, we'll add `SOIL_free_image_data()` function for that we merely specify our image character array.
20. Then, we're going to unbind the texture using `glBindTexture()` function and to that function we'll pass `GL_TEXTURE_2D`, and we'll unbind the texture by passing 0. Have a look at the following code for a clear understanding:

```
//Generate mipmaps
glGenerateMipmap( GL_TEXTURE_2D );
SOIL_free_image_data( image );
glBindTexture( GL_TEXTURE_2D, 0 );
```

You might be thinking what is a mipmap? A mipmap is essentially a level of detail scheme for texture image. It's a way of creating a bunch of small images by a factor of 2 of the original image, and then loading the one that is the closest to the actual texture being displayed at any given point, depending on the distance from the viewer. So if something's further away, the texture required isn't as big. Whereas if it's nearer, it requires a bigger texture. So, it just helps in loading the texture properly. It is recommended to have a quick check on the internet to understand mipmapping a bit more.

We're not done with our code yet. So, we'll move on to our while loop now

Modifying the while loop

Let's follow the below mentioned steps:

1. In the while loop we'll put some code between the point where we're using the shader and where we're binding the vertex array. What we want to do here is add `glActiveTexture()` function. This function will help us activating the texture that we specify.
2. Then, we'll add function `glBindTexture()`. And for this function, we pass `GL_TEXTURE_2D` and `texture`.
3. Next, we just add `glUniform1i()` function and pass to it the following highlighted parameters.

    ```
    // Draw the triangle
    ourShader.Use( );
    glActiveTexture( GL_TEXTURE0 );
    glBindTexture( GL_TEXTURE_2D, texture );
    glUniform1i( glGetUniformLocation( ourShader.Program, "ourTexture" ), 0 );
    ```

4. Then we'll add the code to draw our container:

    ```
    // Draw container
    glBindVertexArray( VAO );
    glDrawElements( GL_TRIANGLES, 6, GL_UNSIGNED_INT, 0 );
    glBindVertexArray( 0 );
    ```

Drawing Shapes and Applying Textures

5. And the last thing that we need to do is just delete the buffer for the element buffer object. So, we'll add `glDeleteBuffers( 1, &EBO );` to our code:

    ```
    // Properly de-allocate all resources once they've outlived their
    purpose
    glDeleteVertexArrays( 1, &VAO );
    glDeleteBuffers( 1, &VBO );
    glDeleteBuffers( 1, &EBO );

    // Terminate GLFW, clearing any resources allocated by GLFW.
    glfwTerminate( );
    ```

And now, if we run our code. There will be some error in the compilation of the code and you will get the output similar to the following image:

This is not what we intended; this is obviously not what we wanted to load in our shape. So, let's try to understand the reason behind this. The only reason we are getting the wrong output is because we have not updated our vertex and fragment shaders for loading the texture. So let's update it.

Chapter 2

Updating the shader files to integrate texture coordinates

Follow these steps to carry out the modifications in your shader files:

1. First, let's go to the vertex shader, our `core.vs` file, and make the changes highlighted in the following code:

   ```
   #version 330 core
   layout (location = 0) in vec3 position;
   layout (location = 1) in vec3 color;
   layout (location = 2) in vec2 texCoord;
   out vec3 ourColor;
   out vec2 TexCoord;
   void main()
   {
    gl_Position = vec4(position, 1.0f);
    ourColor = color;
    // We swap the y-axis by substracing our coordinates from 1. This
   is done because most images have the top y-axis inversed with
   OpenGL's top y-axis.
    // TexCoord = texCoord;
    TexCoord = vec2(texCoord.x, 1.0 - texCoord.y);
   }
   ```

   You might be wondering what are we doing here in `TexCoord = vec2(texCoord.x, 1.0 - texCoord.y);`. Well, what we're doing is swapping the y axis by subtracting our coordinates from 1, and this is done simply because most images have the top y-axis inverted in OpenGL.

2. Next, go to the fragment shader, `core.frag`, and make the following highlighted modifications:

   ```
   #version 330 core
   in vec3 ourColor;
   in vec2 TexCoord;
   out vec4 color;
   // Texture samplers
   uniform sampler2D ourTexture1;
   void main()
   {
    // Linearly interpolate between both textures (second texture is
   //only slightly combined)
    color = texture(ourTexture1, TexCoord);
   }
   ```

[75]

Drawing Shapes and Applying Textures

And now, if we save the updated shader file and run our program, we will get the following output:

Check whether your image fit are spot on with the ratio. If it looks a bit squashed, that's simply because of the coordinates that we have defined for the vertices. It's nothing to do with the texture loading. In later chapters, we'll be learning to use logical coordinates, so that any image that you load can fit in properly. So, that is it for texture loading.

Summary

In this chapter, we learned how to draw various shapes using shaders. We began by drawing a triangle and adding color to it. Then, we used the triangle concept to draw our quadrilateral and learned how to apply texture to it.

In the next chapter, we'll learn how to apply transformations such as translation and rotation to our shape, and learn to draw a cube and apply texture to it. We'll also explore the concepts of projections: Perspective and Orthographic, and how to implement those in our world.

3
Transformations, Projections, and Camera

In the previous chapter, we discussed about how to create shapes in OpenGL using our libraries. We learned to add colors to our shapes and we'll also discussed how to add texture to the shapes. This chapter will be the continuation of the previous chapter and we'll discuss how to apply transformations such as rotation or translate to our shapes. We'll also discuss the projection and the coordinate system and try to implement that in our game world. You'll also get to learn about the camera class and we'll use that to view and navigate through our multiple objects we'll create in this chapter.

The following topics will be covered in this chapter:

- Applying transformations such as rotations and translate to our shapes
- Implementation of projection and the coordinate system in the game world
- Adding multiple objects to our game world
- Creating and using camera class for a better view of objects

So let's begin...

> You can refer to all the code files for this chapter in the `Chapter03` folder on GitHub. The GitHub link can be found in the preface of the book.

Transformations using GLM

We'll be looking at making transformations to our shape and the texture applied to it. To do the transformations, we'll be using the OpenGL Mathematics library that is GLM. For transformations, we need to use vectors and matrices, and GLM handles a lot of that in the backend for us. All we have to do is call the correct method (for example, translate or rotate), and it'll do the appropriate matrices and vector transformations for us.

> It is recommended that you go to `learnopengl.com` and `open.gl`. These sites have got some great resources that showcase all the different vectors and matrices and how to use them, and it goes into more depth about the mathematics behind it. So, if you're interested, you should definitely visit these sites.

Setting up a project to use GLM on Windows / Mac

So, to begin with, we need to download and install the GLM library onto our system. It's very similar to installing the other frameworks that we learned to install in the previous chapters, whether it's GLFW, SDL, or SFML. But if you wish to review this, please refer to the *Setting up a project to use SOIL on Windows or Mac* section in `Chapter 2`, *Drawing Shapes and Applying Textures*. The setup process for GLM will be very much similar to what was discussed in the mentioned section. For the further sections we'll assume that you've install the GLM library in your system and set the project up too.

Now that the GLM library is installed and our project is setup, let's move on to make some modifications to our code so that we can transform our shapes and textures applied to it. In further sections, we'll make some modifications to our code from the previous chapter to transform our shapes.

So, to begin with, we will first need to update our shader files.

Updating shader files

Let's follow the below mentioned steps to update the shader files:

1. We'll go to our vertex shader that is `core.vs` file and perform the following highlighted modifications to the code:

    ```
    #version 330 core
    layout (location = 0) in vec3 position;
    layout (location = 1) in vec3 color;
    layout (location = 2) in vec2 texCoord;
    out vec3 ourColor;
    out vec2 TexCoord;

    uniform mat4 transform;

    void main()
    {
     gl_Position = transform * vec4(position, 1.0f);
     ourColor = color;
     TexCoord = vec2(texCoord.x, 1.0 - texCoord.y);
    }
    ```

2. For the fragment shader, we don't need to do anything as we'll be requiring that code as it is.

Now we can go to `main.cpp` and carry out the modification to our main code to apply transformations to our objects.

Applying transformations to the objects

Take a look at the following steps to understand the modifications that we need to carry out to incorporate transformations in our main code:

1. To make changes to our main code, we'll begin by including the GLM header file in our code, so add the following highlighted include terms in your code:

    ```
    #include <glm/glm.hpp>
    #include <glm/gtc/matrix_transform.hpp>
    #include <glm/gtc/type_ptr.hpp>
    ```

2. The next thing that we are going to do is create the transformation matrix that we want to apply. To do this, go to the while loop, and somewhere in the loop between defining the shader and activating the texture we'll need to add the code described as follows:
   1. First of all, we're going to just create the transformation matrix. So, we'll begin by typing `glm::mat4` and we'll call it `transform`.
   2. Then we'll add the type of transformation. For the translate transformation we'll define it as `transform = glm::translate();`. For the `translate ()` function, the first parameter that we will need to specify is the 4x4 matrix that we're going to use. Next, we'll specify the vector, which is `glm::vec3()`. This takes three parameters—the x, y, and z coordinates—and for those we'll pass the values `0.5f`, `-0.5f` and `0.0f`. Remember, the values should range between -1 and 1, for now.
   3. Next, we'll define the rotate transformation, `transform = glm::rotate()`, and for the `rotate()` function we'll pass parameters: for the `matrix`, we're going to specify `transform` again. For the `angle`, we need to state how much we want it to rotate by, because we don't want it just to rotate once. We want it to constantly rotate. Therefore, we'll add `glfwGetTime()` and cast it to `GLfloat`. The `glfwGetTime()` function will be the amount of time that has passed since GLFW was initialized and use that to rotate our object.

> For more information on **time methods**, you can visit the following links: for GLFW time input, visit `https://www.glfw.org/docs/3.0/group__time.html`;
> for SDL time input, you can use the `SDL_GetTicks` method and read the information at `https://wiki.libsdl.org/SDL_GetTicks`; and, for SFML, you can use the `getElapsedTime` method and for more info on that you can visit `https://www.sfml-dev.org/tutorials/2.5/system-time.php`

   We will need to time the method so that the texture rotates at a certain speed. So, we will multiply the method `glfwGetTime( )` by `-5.0f`. This will make the object rotate in one way. If you add a positive number, it rotates the other way. Try experimenting with the value. By increasing the value you will make it rotate faster, and by reducing the value you will make it go slower.

The third parameter that we need to pass is `glm::vec3()`, and for the vector you have to specify what axes you want the shapes to rotate around. So, either use `1.0f` or `0.0f`. Adding `0.0f` means you don't want it to rotate around that particular axis. So, we'll define it as `0.0f, 0.0f, 1.0f`. This means that our texture will rotate around the z axis. The reason we've chosen z is because, at the moment, we're not doing anything in 3D. So, by rotating round the z axis, it'll just look like it's a 2D transformation.

Take a look at the following code to get a clear understanding of the preceding description:

```
// Create transformations
glm::mat4 transform;
transform = glm::translate( transform, glm::vec3( 0.5f, -0.5f, 0.0f ) );
transform = glm::rotate( transform, ( GLfloat)glfwGetTime( ) * -5.0f, glm::vec3( 0.0f, 0.0f, 1.0f ) );
```

3. Now that we've created our transformation matrix, we can actually get on to applying it. Therefore, we need to get the matrix uniform location and set the matrix up for our shader to use. So we need to create a `GLint` variable `transformLocation` and to that we'll assign the value of `glGetUniformLocation()`, and to this function need to pass `ourShader.Program` and our transformation matrix `"transform"`. Next, we need to define uniform matrix in our code, so add the `glUniformMatrix4fv()` function to our code, and this takes a few parameters. First of all is the `transformLocation`, then 1, and then `GL_FALSE` and `glm::value_ptr()`, and to this function we need to specify the transformation matrix that we're using:

```
// Get matrix's uniform location and set matrix
GLint transformLocation = glGetUniformLocation( ourShader.Program, "transform" );
glUniformMatrix4fv( transformLocation, 1, GL_FALSE, glm::value_ptr( transform ) );
```

> If you want to know more about what these parameters are doing, it is recommended that you check out `learnopengl.com` and `open.gl`, because these sites explain a lot of this in more depth.

Transformations, Projections, and Camera

And now we're all set and ready to run. If we run this, we should get our image rotating in the top-right corner, as shown in the following screenshot:

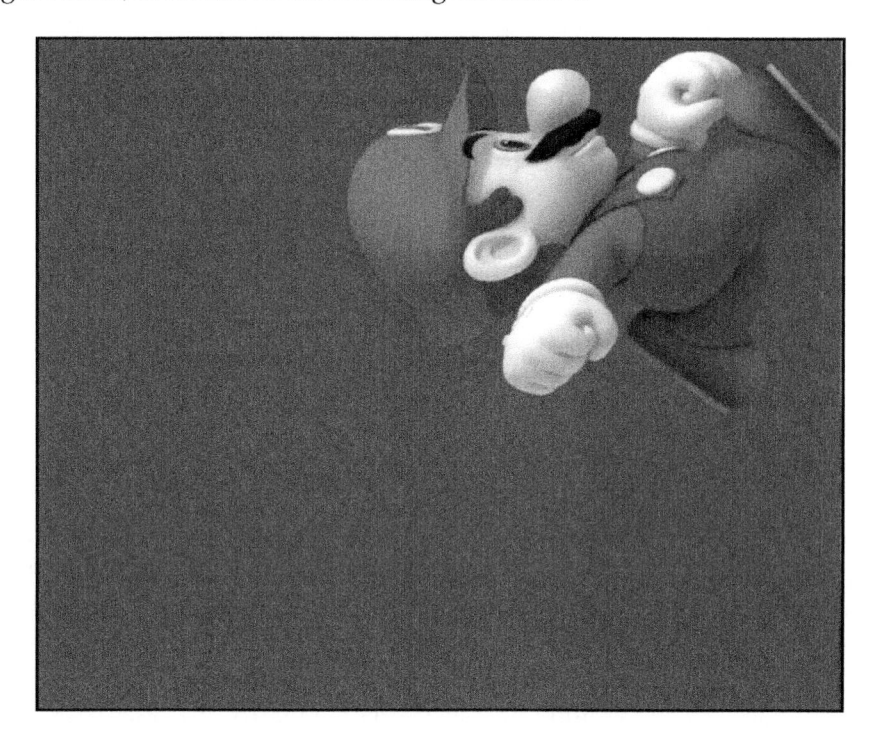

> The illustration used in this chapter is for explanatory purposes only. We do not recommend you to misuse these in any way. For more information please consult the terms and conditions of the publisher mentioned in the Disclaimer section of this book.

It is recommended that you try experimenting with the following line of code to vary the location and speed of rotation:

```
transform = glm::rotate( transform, ( GLfloat)glfwGetTime( ) * -5.0f,
glm::vec3( 0.0f, 0.0f, 1.0f ) );
```

Projections and coordinate systems

In this section, we're going to look at the projections and the coordinate systems. So let's first understand what the coordinate systems are? There are two types of coordinate system: a left-handed and a right-handed coordinate system. The best way to visualize them is to put up both of your hands, as shown in the following image:

[82]

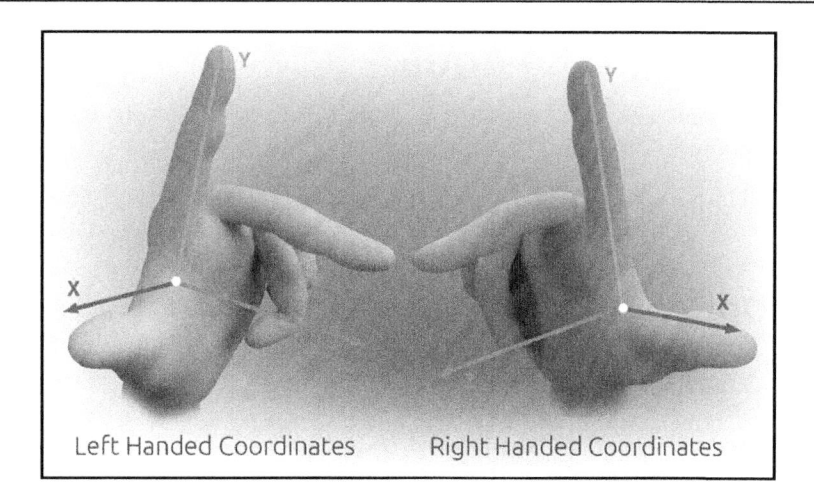

Left Handed Coordinates   Right Handed Coordinates

As per the image, the index fingers of both your hands should point up. Your middle fingers should point towards you and your thumbs should point to the left and right directions, respectively. Once you've done that, the direction that your fingers and your thumbs are pointing is the positive direction for that axis. So, the way the index finger is pointing (upward) is the positive y axis. The direction in which the middle finger is pointing is the positive z axis and the thumbs are pointing in the direction of the positive x axis. OpenGL uses the right-handed coordinate system, while the DirectX uses the left-handed coordinate system.

> For more information on the coordinate system, you can check out the following links:
> `https://learnopengl.com/` and `https://open.gl./`

Now that we've discussed the coordinate system, let's understand the different types of projection we've got in OpenGL. We have the perspective projection and orthographic projection. Perspective projection takes depth into consideration, which, generally speaking, every game in production would, whereas, orthographic projection doesn't take depth into consideration. So, in orthographic projection, an object or part of an object that is further away from you still looks the same size. If you have two identical objects and one is further away, it will still look the same size. However, in perspective projection, just like in real life, the object, that is further away would look smaller. You might be wondering, where orthographic projection would ever be useful? One example is in architecture, when you're creating a laid-out design and you want to have objects behind other objects, but, because you're giving measurements, you don't want them to vary in size.

Modifications to the code

In this section, we will make some modifications to our texture code to integrate projection and coordinate system in our game world.

We'll begin our modifications by updating the shader files.

Making modifications to the shader files

Check out the next steps to understand what modifications we need to do to our shader files:

1. The first thing that we want to do is go to our vertex shader and carry out the following highlighted changes to the code:

```
#version 330 core
layout (location = 0) in vec3 position;
layout (location = 2) in vec2 texCoord;
out vec2 TexCoord;
uniform mat4 model;
uniform mat4 view;
uniform mat4 projection;
void main()
{
  gl_Position = projection * view * model * vec4(position, 1.0f);
  TexCoord = vec2(texCoord.x, 1.0   texCoord.y);
}
```

In the preceding code, we have removed all the color values because we are just using textures now. Second, we deleted the uniform matrix transform as well because we're going to use a few different ways of transforming. Third, we created a uniform 4x4 matrix, which is going to be the model matrix. Fourth, we created a uniform 4x4 matrix, which is the view matrix, and another uniform 4x4 matrix, which is the projection matrix. These three different types of matrices do very important stuff. The model matrix converts local-object coordinates to camera coordinates. The projection matrix converts the camera coordinates to normalized coordinates, so the coordinates are between 0 and 1, and the view matrix converts the normalized coordinates to window coordinates. Finally, we assigned the value of multiplication for the matrix to the `gl_position` to implement it.

2. Next, we'll move on to the core-fragment shader, and in here we'll get rid of `vec3 ourColor;` and the rest will remain as it is. The reason for deleting the color parameter is the same as described in the previous step.

Modifications to the main code

Now that we have updated our shader files, we'll go ahead and make some modifications to our main code to implement the projection and the coordinate system. Follow the below mentioned steps:

1. First of all, we'll get rid of the EBO, as we're not using the element buffer object anymore; we'll get rid of any other instances of element buffer object, and we'll remove the `glDeleteBuffers( 1, &EBO )`, too. Then, we'll delete the color attribute.

2. Now that we have cleaned our project, we are going to enable depth in our code; the reason we need to enable it is because if we've got 3D objects or objects that are further away from us or nearer to us, we need to plan for depth. So, let's go to our code and below `glViewport` we'll add the `glEnable()` function; to do this, we'll pass `GL_DEPTH_TEST`. Then, we'll go to the while loop, and in the `glClear()` function we'll need to specify depth to clear the depth buffer, so add `| GL_DEPTH_BUFFER_BIT` to it.

3. Now that we've implemented depth in our application, we're going update the indices and the vertices present in our code. We are implementing a 3D cube in this section to help illustrate perspective and orthographic projection. Therefore, we'll have to make modifications to our vertices and get rid of our indices. To add the updated vertices to your code, please refer to the `main.cpp` present inside the `Projections and Coordinate Systems` folder. You'll observe that there are vertices for two types of projections: orthographic projection and the perspective projection. We'll be switching between the two of them to understand the difference between the two projections. In the updated vertices, we have defined six sets of vertices and texture coordinates, each one for a face of the cube. For your reference, check out a set of vertices for one side of the cube that is mentioned in the following and let's try to understand what it defines:

```
// Positions            //Texture Coordinates
-0.5f, -0.5f, -0.5f,    0.0f, 0.0f,
 0.5f, -0.5f, -0.5f,    1.0f, 0.0f,
 0.5f,  0.5f, -0.5f,    1.0f, 1.0f,
 0.5f,  0.5f, -0.5f,    1.0f, 1.0f,
-0.5f,  0.5f, -0.5f,    0.0f, 1.0f,
-0.5f, -0.5f, -0.5f,    0.0f, 0.0f,
```

In the preceding code, the first three values in a row are the x, y and z positions, and the next two are the normalized texture coordinates. We covered pretty much all of this in the previous section. It is recommended that you take a look at each one of these sets and try to figure out which face of the cube they correlate to.

4. Next, once we've updated the vertices, we need to make some modifications to our attributes, so take look at the updated attributes, as follows, and make similar changes to our code:

```
// Position attribute
  glVertexAttribPointer( 0, 3, GL_FLOAT , GL_FALSE, 5 * sizeof(
GLfloat ), ( GLvoid * )0 );
  glEnableVertexAttribArray( 0 );

// TexCoord attribute
  glVertexAttribPointer( 2, 2, GL_FLOAT, GL_FALSE, 5 * sizeof(
GLfloat ), ( GLvoid * )( 3 * sizeof( GLfloat ) ) );
  glEnableVertexAttribArray( 2 );
```

In the preceding code, we have updated the factor by which we multiply size of vertices to 5 because there are five different pieces of information on each row in our updated vertices.

5. In terms of our texture loading, we won't touch any of that code whatsoever, as that is defining our texture perfectly.
6. So, after we've unbinded the texture and cleaned it up, and before the `while` loop starts, we are going to define the projection matrix `glm::mat4 projection;`, The first one we're going to discuss is perspective projection, because that's the one that you'll probably be using most of the time. Therefore, we'll add `projection = glm::perspective();` the `perspective()` takes a few values:
    - The first value is the field of view, and, for that, we're going to use 45 degrees. This is a very common value for video games.
    - The second value is the aspect ratio, and, for that, we'll add `screenWidth / screenHeight`. This keeps it dynamic. We're going to cast each to `GLfloat`.
    - For the third value (the near clipping plane), we'll just add `0.1f`.
    - For the fourth value (the far clipping plane), we'll use `1000.0f`.

Take a look at the following highlighted code to understand the previous description:

```
// Unbind texture when done, so we won't accidentily mess up our texture.
glBindTexture( GL_TEXTURE_2D, 0 );

glm::mat4 projection;
projection = glm::perspective( 45.0f, ( GLfloat )screenWidth / ( GLfloat )screenHeight, 0.1f, 100.0f );
```

View Frustum

Let's try to understand the preceding description of code with the help of a simple View Frustum image, as follows:

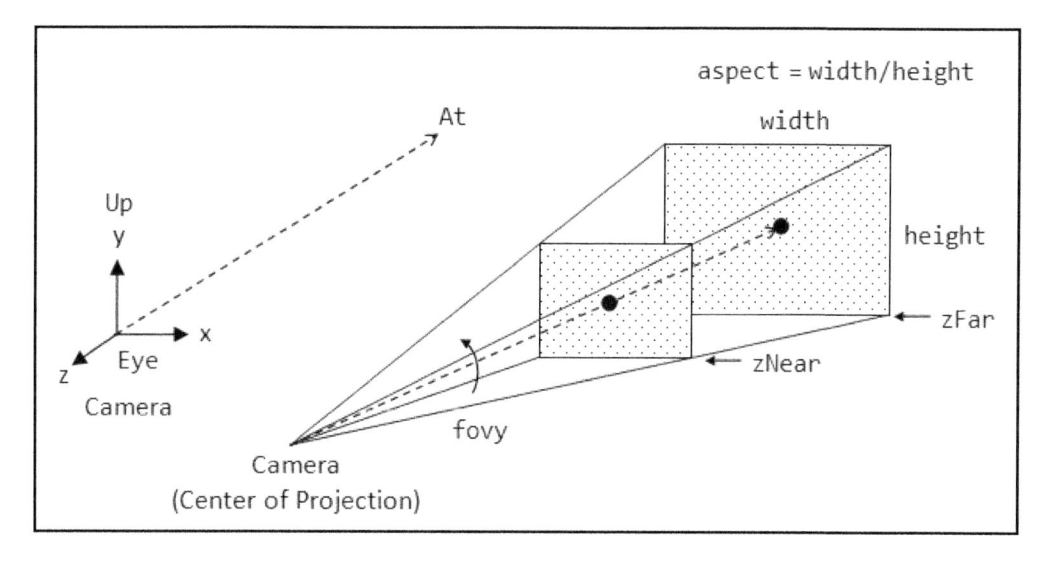

The center of projection is where the virtual camera is placed. **zNear** is the near clipping plane, which we have defined as `0.1f` in our code. The `1000.0f` value refers to the far clipping plane, which is **zFar**. These two values mean that anything nearer than the near clipping plane won't be drawn for you on the screen, anything further than the far clipping plane won't be drawn for you, and anything outside of the view frustum box won't be drawn for you either. The aspect ratio is the **width** divided by the **height**, and the field of view is basically how tall it is.

Transformations, Projections, and Camera

Modifications to while loop

Now that we've created the projection matrix, we can actually start creating the model and the view matrices, and you need to do that within our while loop. Let's take a look at the following steps:

1. So, to begin with, we're going to get rid of the code that defines our transformation matrix, as we're no longer using that. We'll move the `glActiveTexture()` code before we activate our shader.
2. After that, we're going to create the model and view matrices, for which we'll add the following code to our while loop after we have activated our shader. We'll begin with adding the `glm::mat4 model` and `glm::mat4 view` matrix. The model will be `model = glm::rotate()`, and we'll just put an initial sort of rotation in `rotate()`. For the `rotate()`, we're going to pass following parameters:
   - First we'll pass `model`, which refers to the model matrix

```
// Activate shader
ourShader.Use( );

// Create transformations
glm::mat4 model;
glm::mat4 view;
model = glm::rotate( model, ( GLfloat)glfwGetTime( ) * 1.0f,
glm::vec3( 0.5f, 1.0f, 0.0f ) ); // use with perspective projection

//model = glm::rotate( model, 0.5f, glm::vec3( 1.0f, 0.0f, 0.0f )
); // use to compare orthographic and perspective projection
  //view = glm::translate( view, glm::vec3( screenWidth / 2,
screenHeight / 2, -700.0f ) ); // use with orthographic projection

view = glm::translate( view, glm::vec3( 0.0f, 0.0f, -3.0f ) ); //
use with perspective projection
```

Chapter 3

- Second for the angle of rotation, we're just going to pass the `glfwGetTime()`, which will get the time between starting GLFW and now. This is obviously only going to constantly increase, hence we can use this as a nice way of providing rotation. We'll cast this function to `GLfloat`, then we'll multiply it by `1.0f`. This is a great way of increasing and decreasing the speed, as all you have do is vary the value.

> **TIP**
> For more information about angle of rotation, please refer to the information box that was provided earlier with links for SFML, SDL, and GLFW, for you to check out.

- The next parameter that we're going to provide is the vector 3 matrix `glm::vec3()`, and for `vec3()` we're going to use `0.5f` in the x axis, `1.0f` in the y axis and we're not going to have any rotation in the z axis. This is going to add a nice effect to our cube.

3. Next, we are going to type `view = glm::translate()`. In here, we're going to move the view slightly. So, in the `translate ()`, we'll first pass our view matrix; then we specify what sort of movement we want, so will type `glm::vec3()` ; and to `vec3()` we're going to pass `0.0f, 0.0f, -3.0f` for the axes. So we're going to be moving the camera, which is essentially so we can actually see what is going on. Otherwise, we'd principally be within our cube only.

Take a look at the following code to understand the preceding description:

```
// Create transformations
view = glm::translate( view, glm::vec3( 0.0f, 0.0f, -3.0f ) ); // use with perspective projection
```

Now that we've got that sorted, you might be wondering why we are adding a rotation and a translation matrix. This is just for this particular section to get a better view of the projections. You may not want to add a rotation or a translation matrix to further sections.

Transformations, Projections, and Camera

4. Next, to get the uniform location, we'll add following highlighted lines of code:

   ```
   // Get their uniform location
   GLint modelLoc = glGetUniformLocation( ourShader.Program, "model" );
   GLint viewLoc = glGetUniformLocation( ourShader.Program, "view" );
   GLint projLoc = glGetUniformLocation( ourShader.Program, "projection" );
   // Pass them to the shaders
   glUniformMatrix4fv( modelLoc, 1, GL_FALSE, glm::value_ptr( model ) );
   glUniformMatrix4fv( viewLoc, 1, GL_FALSE, glm::value_ptr( view ) );
   glUniformMatrix4fv( projLoc, 1, GL_FALSE, glm::value_ptr( projection ) );
   ```

5. Next, we need to draw our object, so we're going to add `glBindVertexArray()`, and to that we'll pass the the vertex array object `VAO`.

6. We'll then add `glDrawArrays ()` to that, firstly, we'll pass:
   - Firstly `GL_TRIANGLES`.
   - Secondly, the first vertex will start at 0
   - For the count we'll pass 36, because there are two triangles per face and each triangle has three coordinates. The two triangles result in six coordinates, so 6 x 6 = 36.

7. Next, we'll unbind it, so we're going to add `glBindVertexArray()` to which we'll pass 0.

   ```
   // Draw container
   glBindVertexArray( VAO );
   glDrawArrays( GL_TRIANGLES, 0, 36 );
   glBindVertexArray( 0 );
   ```

Now we are all sorted, let's recheck the code once and then run it. If you don't come across any errors, you will get a similar rotating cube on your screen to the following:

Orthgraphic projection

Now let's just see how orthgraphic projection looks, and understand the difference between orthographic and perspective projections. So, we're going to comment the perspective-projection coordinates and add the orthagraphic-projection coordinates from the `main.cpp` present inside the `Projections and Coordinate Systems` folder.

Transformations, Projections, and Camera

Then we'll go to our `glm::mat4 projection;` and comment out the perspective projection, and add the following highlighted line of code for the orthographic projection:

```
projection = glm::ortho(0.0f, ( GLfloat )screenWidth, 0.0f, ( GLfloat )screenHeight, 0.1f, 1000.0f);
```

You may be wondering where the field of view and the ratio are. We don't need those because the cube is more like the box shown in the following image:

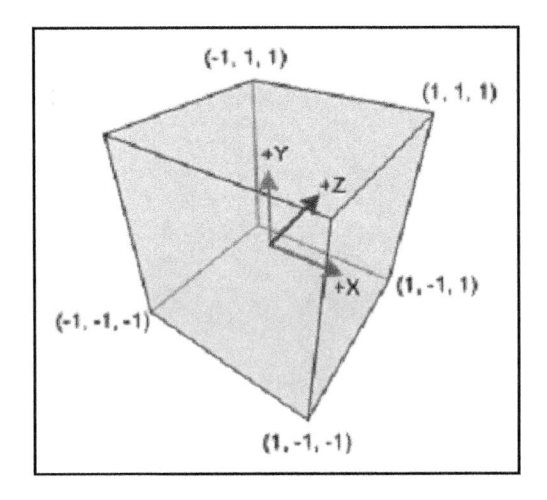

Now we've only other two things that needs to be changed, those are the model and the view matrices, simply because this will help to demonstrate what we're trying to show. So, comment out the perspective-projection model and view definitions, and add the following lines of code:

```
model = glm::rotate( model, 0.5f, glm::vec3( 1.0f, 0.0f, 0.0f ) );
// use to compare orthographic and perspective projection

view = glm::translate( view, glm::vec3( screenWidth / 2, screenHeight / 2, -700.0f ) );
// use with orthographic projection
```

[92]

Now, let's run this code and see what our cube looks like:

So we've got our cube, but this looks a bit weird. It just looks like a big, long rectangle. But what's actually happening is that the image facing us is the front face of the cube and the top rectangular image is the top face of the cube. We've rotated the cube, but without perspective, and it's hard to tell which face is which. But let's try an experiment and watch what happens when we comment out the orthographic `view` and uncomment the perspective `view`. Let's bring in the perspective projection again, uncomment the perspective array, and comment out the orthagraphic array. Now if we run the code with the perspective projection, you'll see a key difference between orthographic and perspective projections; take a look at the following image:

Looking at the preceding image now, it blatantly looks more like a cube. Obviously, we can't see the sides, the bottom, or the back face, but, based on what we're seeing here, it looks much more like a cube compared to how it looked before.

Adding a Camera class to the project

In the previous section, we learned how to add objects to our screen and how to apply texture, transformation and projection to the objects. As we progress ahead in the book, we will add various objects to our screen, but as we add more objects to it and if we wish to view those from different angles, we don't want to have specific code to be able to do that or to move freely around the objects. Therefore, in this chapter, we'll be looking at implementing a `Camera` class, which will help us to move around our world freely, using the keyboard, and view those objects from different angles. Implementing this class will help us to improvise a walking style of movement and take a look at the virtual world around the player with the help of the mouse. As we learned in the previous chapter, what we've got currently is the single cube we've created. As we are seeking to implement multiple objects in this chapter, we'll basically get rid of the vertices that describe our single cube, and use a simple array of vertices and a loop to draw multiple cubes. Instead of just moving around one cube, we'll see multiple cubes, which will be fantastic.

Here are the things we're going to cover in this section:

- Learning how to draw multiple cubes
- Creating the `Camera` class and implementing it in our current application

There are just a few prerequisites before we get started. We'll use the source code from the previous chapter, which was on projections and coordinate systems. If you don't have the source code, you can download it from the GitHub link provided in the preface of this book. Also, in this chapter, we'll be using GLFW as the framework. This means we will be using some GLFW coding here, but this is actually only for the input of what we're doing. Feel free to check out the input guides for other libraries too, try to swap the code with other libraries, and try experimenting. The `Camera` class that we are going to define in this chapter won't be affected by your experimentation, as it isn't going to have any framework-specific code. Only the main code will be affected, as it's going to be used to detect the input.

Let's get started.

Creating a Camera.h header file

We'll begin by creating a header file for our `Camera` class, so we'll create an empty header file in our project and add it to our target. We'll name it `Camera.h`. We'll only have a header because the methods that we're going to implement are very simple methods. But you can extract it into a separate CPP file if you want to. It is recommended that you try experimenting that way as well, because it will be a great way to learn. Let's begin coding our camera header. Follow these steps:

1. First, let's get rid of the default code that is already present in the file. Then, add `#pragma` when the code is a simpler version. This doesn't work on all compilers, but most compilers will support this.
2. Then, we'll add the `#include` vector. We'll be using the `vector` class for stuff such as positioning. Let's then add `#define GLEW_STATIC`, because we're going to be using GLEW in here, which we've already linked to our project. Next, we'll add `#include GL/glew.h`. We're also going to include some OpenGL Mathematics libraries, so let's add `glm/glm.hpp` and `#include glm/gtc/matrix_transform.hpp`.
3. Next, we're going to create an enumeration to define several possible options for camera movement. Let's add `enum Camera_Movements`. This will contain `FORWARD`, `BACKWARD`, `LEFT` and `RIGHT`, which we need to use to find out which way the user wants to move the camera -- essentially, to identify which way a user wants to walk.

Transformations, Projections, and Camera

4. Now, we're going to create some constant camera values for the yaw, pitch, and speed of the camera movement, and sensitivity and zoom. We're not going to have methods for these, apart from for the zoom, but you can have methods for all the other ones. You can create getters and setters; it is recommended that you do this as an extra task. It's a great way of learning and you'll be able to use them later on.

5. So, we're going to add `const`. Obviously, at the moment, because we're using a constant, you won't be able to modify it, but if you do want to modify it, that's not a problem. But these are the default values, so you wouldn't be manipulating this particular variable specifically. You'd be manipulating the variables within the Camera class, which we're going to create in a short while. So, add `const GLfloat YAW = -90.0f;`. Then add `const GLfloat PITCH = 0.0f` and `const GLfloat SPEED = 6.0f`. This is the value of speed that we've discovered works well with the camera and screen; you can manipulate it to make it slower and faster, as you desire. A higher value is faster and a lower value is slower. Next, add `const GLfloat SENSITIVITY = 0.25f`. This defines the sensitivity of our mouse movement. Again, the higher the value, the faster the mouse movement, and the lower the value, the slower the mouse movement. Now we're going to include `const GLfloat ZOOM`. The zoom value is the field of view, so a value of 45 degrees is very common. A higher value would basically mean a taller screen. It's essentially what the old games used, so you can try that. Check out the following code to understand the preceding description:

```
#pragma once
// Std. Includes
#include <vector>
// GL Includes
#define GLEW_STATIC
#include <GL/glew.h>

#include <glm/glm.hpp>
#include <glm/gtc/matrix_transform.hpp>

// Defines several possible options for camera movement. Used as
abstraction to stay away from window-system specific input methods
enum Camera_Movement
{
    FORWARD,
    BACKWARD,
    LEFT,
    RIGHT
};
```

```
// Default camera values
const GLfloat YAW        = -90.0f;
const GLfloat PITCH      = 0.0f;
const GLfloat SPEED      = 6.0f;
const GLfloat SENSITIVTY = 0.25f;
const GLfloat ZOOM       = 45.0f;
```

6. Next, we're going to create a Camera class and then type `public`. We're going to create a constructor with vectors first, and then a constructor with scalar values. Let's begin by adding `Camera ()`, which will take the parameters shown in the following code:

```
//Constructor with vectors
Camera( glm::vec3 position = glm::vec3( 0.0f, 0.0f, 0.0f ),
glm::vec3 up = glm::vec3( 0.0f, 1.0f, 0.0f ), GLfloat yaw = YAW,
GLfloat pitch = PITCH ) : front( glm::vec3( 0.0f, 0.0f, -1.0f ) ),
movementSpeed( SPEED ), mouseSensitivity( SENSITIVTY ), zoom( ZOOM
)
```

7. Then, we're going to quickly implement our camera constructor, so add the following lines for the constructor:

```
{
    this->position = position;
    this->worldUp = up;
    this->yaw = yaw;
    this->pitch = pitch;
    this->updateCameraVectors( );
}
```

8. Now that we're done with this particular constructor, we're going to add the constructor with scalar values to our code. Add the following lines to your code:

```
// Constructor with scalar values
    Camera( GLfloat posX, GLfloat posY, GLfloat posZ, GLfloat upX,
GLfloat upY, GLfloat upZ, GLfloat yaw, GLfloat pitch ) : front(
glm::vec3( 0.0f, 0.0f, -1.0f ) ), movementSpeed( SPEED ),
mouseSensitivity( SENSITIVTY ), zoom( ZOOM )
    {
        this->position = glm::vec3( posX, posY, posZ );
        this->worldUp = glm::vec3( upX, upY, upZ );
        this->yaw = yaw;
        this->pitch = pitch;
        this->updateCameraVectors( );
    }
```

Transformations, Projections, and Camera

9. Now we're going to implement a getter for getting the view matrix, because this'll return the view matrix that is calculated using Euler angles and the `lookAt` matrix. We're going to add `glm::mat4`, and we're going to call it `GetViewMatrix( )`. We'll use this in our `main.cpp`, and we'll add the following highlighted line of code to that class:

   ```
   // Returns the view matrix calculated using Eular Angles and the
   LookAt Matrix
       glm::mat4 GetViewMatrix( )
       {
            return glm::lookAt( this->position, this->position +
   this->front, this->up );
       }
   ```

   This is basically just stating where we want to look; we want to be looking in front, obviously; and we want to use the up vector so we've made it relative.

10. Now we're going to just process some keyboard input; using this keyboard input, we'll detect if we're going forward, backward, left, or right, and we'll move in that direction. So let's add the following line of code:

    ```
    void ProcessKeyboard( Camera_Movement direction, GLfloat deltaTime
    )    {
    ```

    This `Camera_Movement` is the `enum` that we created in the preceding steps. `GLfloat deltaTime` is the time between frames, so we can create frame-independent movement, because the last thing you want is to have 60 frames per second and suddenly dip to 30 frames, which is half the speed. You want it to be the same speed, obviously. It won't look as smooth, but you'll still get a consistent movement, and that is what is important.

11. Next, in the code file, we're going to add the following lines of code:

    ```
    // Processes input received from any keyboard-like input system.
    Accepts input parameter in the form of camera defined ENUM (to
    abstract it from windowing systems)
        void ProcessKeyboard( Camera_Movement direction, GLfloat
    deltaTime )
        {
            GLfloat velocity = this->movementSpeed * deltaTime;

            if ( direction == FORWARD )
            {
                this->position += this->front * velocity;
            }
    ```

```
        if ( direction == BACKWARD )
        {
            this->position -= this->front * velocity;
        }

        if ( direction == LEFT )
        {
            this->position -= this->right * velocity;
        }

        if ( direction == RIGHT )
        {
            this->position += this->right * velocity;
        }
    }
```

In the preceding lines of code, we added `GLfloat velocity` and assigned it the value of `movementSpeed * deltaTime`. So, let's say the `movementSpeed` is 5, for example, and the `deltaTime` is `0.1`, so the `GLfloat velocity` would be `0.5`. Hence, if it's a higher delta time, it'll have a higher movement speed. If it's a lower delta time, it'll have a lower movement speed. This just keeps it all frame-rate independent. Next, we added `if` statements to check the direction in which the user is moving. If the user is moving in any particular direction, then the `position += this front * velocity,` where `velocity` is equal to the value that we've already calculated.

You might be wondering why we aren't using a switch statement or why we aren't using an `if else/if else` series. First, let's say you clicked the forward key and the left key, then you want to be able to move essentially in a northwest direction. Ignoring which way we're looking—so let's assume we're just looking north - you want to be able to move northwest. You don't want to have to press one key, then let go, then press another key. Likewise, if you're moving forward and you click backwards, you'll stop. You don't want to be having to release keys; this is the reason we're using separate `if` statements.

Transformations, Projections, and Camera

12. The next thing we'll do is process the mouse movement. This will process the input received from our mouse system, whether that's GLFW, SDL, or SFML, and it will use an offset value so it can adjust the x and y direction. So, we're going to add `void ProcessMouseMovement()` and pass `GLfloat xOffset` to it. This is essentially the difference between the mouse movements, because, otherwise, how do we know where we're moving to? We essentially need to think about the speed. Then add `GLfloat yOffset, GLboolean constrainPitch` to constrain the pitch and set that equal to true. Now we're going to calculate the offset, and we'll adjust that using our `mouseSensitivity`. We'll add the following lines of code:

    ```
    xOffset *= this->mouseSensitivity;
    yOffset *= this->mouseSensitivity;

    this->yaw   += xOffset;
    this->pitch += yOffset;
    ```

13. Now, we're going to check if the pitch is constrained by using the if statement. We want to prevent the user from being able to go out of bounds, so that the screen doesn't get flipped if we move our mouse, or effectively the way we look, to the left and to the right; if we move to the left for too long, we'll loop back round. The same is true for the right direction (that is, anti-clockwise and clockwise. When you look up and down, you generally only want to be able to look up by about 90 degrees, which is roughly what your head can do, and then just look down by roughly 90 degrees to your feet, which is again approximately what your head can do. You don't want to be able to just keep looping back round, because you'll start getting all sorts of different problems, such as gimbal lock. But, in general, that's not the sort of movement that you have in games, because games are based on real life and the constraints of the human body. So we're going to check the pitch. If `pitch > 89.0f`, then we'll assign the pitch as `89.0f`. If `pitch < -89.0f`, we'll assign the pitch as `-89.0f`. Finally, we'll update the camera vectors by adding `this->updateCameraVectors( );`. This will update the front, right, and up vectors using the Euler angles that we've defined here. Take a look at the following code to understand the preceding description:

    ```
    // Processes input received from a mouse input system. Expects the
    offset value in both the x and y direction.
        void ProcessMouseMovement( GLfloat xOffset, GLfloat yOffset,
    GLboolean constrainPitch = true )
        {
            xOffset *= this->mouseSensitivity;
            yOffset *= this->mouseSensitivity;
    ```

```
        this->yaw   += xOffset;
        this->pitch += yOffset;

        // Make sure that when pitch is out of bounds, screen
doesn't get flipped
        if ( constrainPitch )
        {
            if ( this->pitch > 89.0f )
            {
                this->pitch = 89.0f;
            }
            if ( this->pitch < -89.0f )
            {
                this->pitch = -89.0f;
            }
        }

        // Update Front, Right and Up Vectors using the updated
Eular angles
        this->updateCameraVectors( );
    }
```

14. Now that we've processed the mouse movement, we're going to process the mouse scroll, so we'll add `void ProcessMouseScroll()`, and we'll pass `GLfloat yOffset` to that.

    You can use `xOffset` if you want to be able to detect the horizontal scroll. A lot of mice don't have horizontal scroll, but quite a few new mice, especially gaming mice and productivity mice, do. But, generally speaking, you probably only want to detect movement in the y axis--that is, vertical scroll. But you can easily extend this method, and this class in general, to suit your requirements.

    Add the following `if` statements to your code:

```
    if ( this->zoom >= 1.0f && this->zoom <= 45.0f )
        {
            this->zoom -= yOffset;
        }

        if ( this->zoom <= 1.0f )
        {
            this->zoom = 1.0f;
        }

        if ( this->zoom >= 45.0f )
        {
            this->zoom = 45.0f;
```

```
        }
```

Now, we're going to create a getter for getting the zoom, because the zoom variable will be private. Actually, all the variables are private in this class. We're only really creating the zoom getter simply because it's the only one we're using outside of this class for now. But if you need to use something such as the up vector, the yaw, the pitch, or any of the other variables that we're creating, feel free to create appropriate getters and setters. Therefore, we'll next add following code:

```
GLfloat GetZoom( )
    {
        return this->zoom;
    }
```

15. Now we're going to do define the camera attributes, so we'll add following lines of code to our camera class:

```
private:
    // Camera Attributes
    glm::vec3 position;
    glm::vec3 front;
    glm::vec3 up;
    glm::vec3 right;
    glm::vec3 worldUp;
```

> Feel free to visit learnopengl.com and open.gl, and check out those websites for more in-depth written information and some nice diagrams regarding all the different variables and the methods that we have discussed in this chapter.

16. Then we'll add some Euler angles to our class:

```
// Eular Angles
    GLfloat yaw;
    GLfloat pitch;
```

17. All of these parameters that we've been using are finally getting created. Next, we'll add some camera options to our code:

```
// Camera options
    GLfloat movementSpeed;
    GLfloat mouseSensitivity;
    GLfloat zoom;
```

18. The last thing we need to add into this class is `void updateCameraVectors`, and, when we're updating the camera vectors, we need to calculate the new front vector, so we'll add `glm::vec3 front`, which is temporary storage for it. Then we'll add `front.x`, and we'll assign a value of `cos ( glm::radians( this->yaw ))` multiplied by `cos( glm::radians( this->pitch ) )` to it. Again, the mathematical calculations here are obviously quite complex and quite in depth, so we would recommend you check out the aforementioned links. Take a look at the following code to understand what other elements will be added to `updateCameraVectors`:

```cpp
void updateCameraVectors( )
{
    // Calculate the new Front vector
    glm::vec3 front;
    front.x = cos( glm::radians( this->yaw ) ) * cos( glm::radians( this->pitch ) );
    front.y = sin( glm::radians( this->pitch ) );
    front.z = sin( glm::radians( this->yaw ) ) * cos( glm::radians( this->pitch ) );
    this->front = glm::normalize( front );
    // Also re-calculate the Right and Up vector
    this->right = glm::normalize( glm::cross( this->front, this->worldUp ) );   // Normalize the vectors, because their length gets closer to 0 the more you look up or down which results in slower movement.
    this->up = glm::normalize( glm::cross( this->right, this->front ) );
}
```

With this last line of code, we have finally completed the `Camera` class. Please check out the `camera.h` file for the entire code. This file is present inside the `camera` folder in the `Getting started` folder.

Making modifications to main.cpp

Now that we have created our `Camera` class, let's go back to our `main.cpp` and make some modifications to it, such as implementing multiple cubes on our screens, adding a camera class, and moving through the multiple objects.

Transformations, Projections, and Camera

In our `main.cpp`, we'll start implementing the input stuff that we've been doing. So, we're going to use the GLFW for our input system, but, again, feel free to check out the previous links for more information on the GLFW, SFML, and SDL input systems.

1. We'll begin with including our `Camera` class in our code. Add `#include Camera.h` at the start of the code,
2. Then, in the section where we define our screen dimensions, we'll make the following modifications:

   ```
   const GLuint WIDTH = 800, HEIGHT = 600;
   int SCREEN_WIDTH, SCREEN_HEIGHT;
   ```

3. Now, let's just replace every `screenWidth` and `screenHeight` we've used with `SCREEN_WIDTH`, and `SCREEN_HEIGHT`.
4. As we'll be using perspective projection, we need to get rid of all the orthographic projection code as we're not using that anymore.
5. Now, before we start with our `int main`, we're going to create some function prototypes. Add the following lines of code to your `main.cpp` file:

   ```
   // Function prototypes
   void KeyCallback( GLFWwindow *window, int key, int scancode, int
   action, int mode );
   void ScrollCallback( GLFWwindow *window, double xOffset, double
   yOffset );
   void MouseCallback( GLFWwindow *window, double xPos, double yPos );
   void DoMovement( );
   ```

   In the preceding code, we first added `void KeyCallback( );` this is where the framework-specific code starts. To that function we passed `GLFWwindow *window`, and then we needed to check what key was pressed, so we added `int key`, `scancode`, `action` and `mode`. We then added the rest of the functions. In the `MouseCallback( )`, we passed `double xPos` and `double yPos`. These are the x and y positions of our mouse in our window. We're actually going to hide the mouse cursor to provide a more immersive experience. Then, we added one final method prototype to the preceding code: `void DoMovement`. This method will be called in every single frame, and this'll move our camera. Even if we haven't made any movement, it'll still be called, but it won't obviously move our camera.

6. Now, we just need to initially set some values up for our camera, so we're going to add `Camera`, create a `camera ( )` object, and we'll pass `glm::vec3 ( )` to it. To the `vec3( )`, we'll pass `0.0f, 0.0f, 3.0f`. These are just the initial values. Next, we'll add `GLfloat lastX`, which is the last position of the camera, initially. We'll make it equal to the center of the screen, so this is going to be our mouse movement. We'll add `WIDTH / 2.0` and `GLfloat lastY = WIDTH / 2.0f;`. Take a look at the following to understand this description:

   ```
   // Camera
   Camera   camera(glm::vec3( 0.0f, 0.0f, 3.0f ) );
   GLfloat lastX = WIDTH / 2.0;
   GLfloat lastY = HEIGHT / 2.0;
   ```

   Below this will be a `bool` of keys, which will be an array of 1,024 different types of key. We're going to add `bool firstMouse = true`, as we're handling one type of mouse:

   ```
   bool keys[1024];
   bool firstMouse = true;
   ```

   Next, we will add `deltatime` and `lastframe`, which will be used in the code to determine the time between frames:

   ```
   GLfloat deltaTime = 0.0f;
   GLfloat lastFrame = 0.0f;
   ```

7. Now, in our int main, after our `glfwMakeContextCurrent( window );` we are going to add `glfwSetKeyCallback( );` and to that we'll provide `window`; we'll provide the method that we're using, which is `KeyCallback`; and then we'll duplicate this line of code three times and make following highlighted modifications to it:

   ```
   // Set the required callback functions
   glfwSetKeyCallback( window, KeyCallback );
   glfwSetCursorPosCallback( window, MouseCallback );
   glfwSetScrollCallback( window, ScrollCallback );
   ```

   Here, we are calling the function prototypes that we have defined previously.

Transformations, Projections, and Camera

8. Next, we want to fix our mouse to the center of our screen, within the window itself, so we'll add `glfwSetInputMode( )` and we'll pass `window` to it. As the mode that we're changing is the cursor, we'll pass `GLFW_CURSOR` with a value of `GLFW_CURSOR_ DISABLED` to it, as we don't want the cursor to be totally disabled.

   ```
   // Options, removes the mouse cursor for a more immersive
   experience     glfwSetInputMode( window, GLFW_CURSOR,
   GLFW_CURSOR_DISABLED );
   ```

9. As we are going to render multiple cubes in this code, we'll create an array of vectors, which will contain the cubes' positions. These are just arbitrary positions, so you can change them later to experiment with those. Go to the `main.cpp` file in the `Camera` folder, and copy and paste the array of vectors `glm::vec3 cubePositions[]` to your code.

   Next, we're going to move the projection code inside the while loop, because we're going to change the field of view using the mouse scroll, so we want to be able to update the projection every single frame if we're actually changing the field-of-view value. So, after we've activated our shader code and binded texture using texture units, add the projection code and make the following changes to it:

   ```
   // Draw our first triangle

       ourShader.Use( );

       // Bind Textures using texture units
       glActiveTexture( GL_TEXTURE0 );
       glBindTexture( GL_TEXTURE_2D, texture );
       glUniform1i( glGetUniformLocation( ourShader.Program,
   "ourTexture1" ), 0 );

       glm::mat4 projection;
       projection = glm::perspective(camera.GetZoom( ),
   (GLfloat)SCREEN_WIDTH/(GLfloat)SCREEN_HEIGHT, 0.1f, 1000.0f);
   ```

Chapter 3

10. After the start of the while loop, we'll set the frame time, so we'll add `GLfloat currentFrame = glfwGetTime()`. Then we'll add `deltaTime = currentFrame - lastFrame`. This is our way of detecting the time between the frames. If, let's say, our current frame is at time 100 and our last frame was at time 80, the time between the last frame and the current frame would be 20-- though it'd normally be a second or millisecond. Then we'll add `lastFrame = the currentFrame`, as the last frame will be the current frame when we restart this while loop on the next iteration, because we'll have a different frame at that particular moment. Refer to the following code to understand the description:

    ```
    while( !glfwWindowShouldClose( window ) )
       {

            // Set frame time
            GLfloat currentFrame = glfwGetTime( );
            deltaTime = currentFrame - lastFrame;
            lastFrame = currentFrame;
    ```

11. After we've handled all the events, we're actually going to handle the movement, so add `DoMovement()`.

12. Now we'll go to the section in the code where we have defined the `view` and model matrix, and make the following modifications:

    ```
    // Create camera transformation
         glm::mat4 view;
         view = camera.GetViewMatrix( );
    ```

    In the preceding code, you must have noticed that we got rid of model-matrix code, which is because we're going to put that inside a for loop that will iterate over our cube-position array, draw the objects in different locations, and use the model to generate sort of a random rotation.

13. Between binding the vertex array to the vertex-array object, and unbinding it, we're essentially going to add a for loop in which we're going to pass a parameter as `GLuint i = 0; i < 10; i++`. It is recommended that you to try to make it dynamic, so you can add more cube positions and you can draw more cubes. That'd be another great task for you. We'll add the following highlighted statements to the for loop. First of all, we're going to calculate the model matrix for each object, and then pass it to our shader before we start drawing:

    ```
    for( GLuint i = 0; i < 10; i++ )
         {
              // Calculate the model matrix for each object and pass
      it to shader before drawing
    ```

[107]

Transformations, Projections, and Camera

```
            glm::mat4 model;
            model = glm::translate( model, cubePositions[i] );
            GLfloat angle = 20.0f * i;
            model = glm::rotate(model, angle, glm::vec3( 1.0f,
    0.3f, 0.5f ) );
            glUniformMatrix4fv( modelLoc, 1, GL_FALSE,
    glm::value_ptr( model ) );

            glDrawArrays( GL_TRIANGLES, 0, 36 );
        }
```

We used a value of 20.0 in the preceding code as it's just a calculated value. Try varying this value and see what happens. You might find a better value than that. We have cut and pasted the glUniformMatrix4fv(); from the while loop. Now we are done with our while loop.

14. Now we can start to implement those function prototypes, which is the last thing to do before we can run the code and observe our output. After the end of while loop, we'll add void DoMovement(), which is going to handle our movement and call the appropriate keyboard method in our Camera class. So, this is not going to take in any parameters, but we will add some if statements. We want to use the W, A, S, D and arrow keys, so we're going to pass the condition as keys[GLFW_KEY_W] || keys[GLFW_KEY_UP]. In the if statement, we'll add camera.ProcessKeyboard(FORWARD, deltaTime); because we're moving forward, and we'll add deltaTime, which we've already calculated in our while loop. This is the code for moving forward. Similarly, we'll add statements for all other directions; take a look at the following highlighted code:

```
// Moves/alters the camera positions based on user input
void DoMovement( )
{
    // Camera controls
    if( keys[GLFW_KEY_W] || keys[GLFW_KEY_UP] )
    {
        camera.ProcessKeyboard( FORWARD, deltaTime );
    }

    if( keys[GLFW_KEY_S] || keys[GLFW_KEY_DOWN] )
    {
        camera.ProcessKeyboard( BACKWARD, deltaTime );
    }

    if( keys[GLFW_KEY_A] || keys[GLFW_KEY_LEFT] )
    {
        camera.ProcessKeyboard( LEFT, deltaTime );
```

Chapter 3

```
    }
    if( keys[GLFW_KEY_D] || keys[GLFW_KEY_RIGHT] )
    {
        camera.ProcessKeyboard( RIGHT, deltaTime );
    }
}
```

15. Then, we're going to do a callback, so we'll add the following code:

```
// Is called whenever a key is pressed/released via GLFW
void KeyCallback( GLFWwindow *window, int key, int scancode, int action, int mode )
{
    if( key == GLFW_KEY_ESCAPE && action == GLFW_PRESS )
    {
        glfwSetWindowShouldClose(window, GL_TRUE);
    }
    if ( key >= 0 && key < 1024 )
    {
        if( action == GLFW_PRESS )
        {
            keys[key] = true;
        }
        else if( action == GLFW_RELEASE )
        {
            keys[key] = false;
        }
    }
}
```

16. Now we can add the `MouseCallback`:

```
void MouseCallback( GLFWwindow *window, double xPos, double yPos )
{
    if( firstMouse )
    {
        lastX = xPos;
        lastY = yPos;
        firstMouse = false;
    }
    GLfloat xOffset = xPos - lastX;
    GLfloat yOffset = lastY - yPos;   // Reversed since y-coordinates go from bottom to left

    lastX = xPos;
    lastY = yPos;

    camera.ProcessMouseMovement( xOffset, yOffset );
```

Transformations, Projections, and Camera

    }

17. Then we are going to add `void ScrollCallback()`, to which we will pass the following parameters: `GLFWwindow *window, double xOffset, double yOffset`

    Inside that method we are going to add the following code:

    ```
    camera.ProcessMouseScroll( yOffset );
    ```

Now we're ready to see if this works, so run it. Once it has been compiled error free, you'll get to see the following output :

We've created our multiple cubes, and we can look around and move. We can use the *W*, *A*, *S*, and *D* keys and arrow keys to move around. So we can move not just forward and backward, but forward and right, forward and left, back and right, and back and left. What's great about this camera system is the forward is relative to the way we're looking. So, if we look at a particular cube, then press forward, it moves towards our cube. If we try to go through the cube, we'll go through and we'll get to see the inverse of the textures. The reason we can go through it is simply because there's no collision detection.

Summary

In this chapter, we learned how to apply transformations such as rotation to our shape, and learned to draw a cube and apply texture to it. Then, we explored the concepts of projections, Perspective and Orthographic, and implemented those in our game world.

In the next chapter, we'll talk about lighting, its effects and sources of light that we have in OpenGL

4
Effects of lighting, Materials and Lightmaps

In the previous chapter, we discussed how to apply transformations and projections to objects. We also created multiple cubes and a `Camera` class to clearly view and navigate around those objects. In this chapter, we're going to look at lighting. Firstly, we're going to discuss the basics of colors with respect to our objects and the source of light. We'll also discuss creating a vertex shader and a fragment shader, like we had in the previous chapters for our object box. We'll be creating a shader for an actual light source such as a lamp. You'll also learn how to apply materials to your object cube and you will observe the effect light has on those materials.

In this chapter we'll cover the following topics:

- The basics of colors in lighting and lighting effects on objects
- Effect of light on a type of material
- Exploring lightmaps to implement the real-world effects of light on different materials

Lights... camera...action!!

> You can refer to all the code files for this chapter in the `Chapter04` folder on GitHub. The GitHub link can be found in the preface of the book.

Effects of lighting , Materials and Lightmaps

Adding an object and a light source

In this section, will discuss how to apply colors to your cube object. We'll also learn how to create shader files for light and for a source of light such as a lamp. And then we'll learn how to add the cube and the light source to our game world.

So, let's begin by creating new shader files for the light and the lamp.

Creating lighting and lamp shader files

Here we'll learn how to create shader files for a light source and a lamp and explore the code that will go into the vertex shaders and the fragment shaders. Perform the following steps to learn how create these shader files:

1. First of all, for rename `core.vs` and `core.frag` from the previous chapters to `lighting.vs` and `lighting.core`.

2. Now let's begin with the modifications to the code of these newly renamed files. First of all, we'll modify `lighting.vs`. What we're going to do here is get rid of the texture coordinate because we're not going to render a texture in here, and we'll also get rid of the `out texture` variable. Take a look at the following code to understand the changes made in the vertex shader for lighting:

   ```
   #version 330 core
   layout (location = 0) in vec3 position;

   uniform mat4 model;
   uniform mat4 view;
   uniform mat4 projection;

   void main()
   {
     gl_Position = projection * view * model * vec4(position, 1.0f);
   }
   ```

3. Next, we'll go to `lighting.frag` and carry out the modifications as in the following code:

   ```
   #version 330 core
   out vec4 color;

   uniform vec3 objectColor;
   uniform vec3 lightColor;
   ```

[114]

```
void main()
{
    color = vec4(lightColor * objectColor, 1.0f);
}
```

In the preceding code, `objectColor`, the variable that we have added, will contain the color of the object itself, which is the cube in our example.

4. Save both the files, and now we'll create shader files for our lamp.

Creating shader files for the lamp

Take a look at the following steps to see how to create lamp shaders:

1. Duplicate the files that we've updated in the preceding steps and rename them `lamp.vs` and `lamp.frag`, and we'll need to modify some code in these new files to create our light source.
2. We won't be making any modifications to `lamp.vs` as we need the updated code as it is.
3. We need to make some modifications to `lamp.frag`, so take a look at the highlighted terms in the following code:

   ```
   #version 330 core
   out vec4 color;

   void main()
   {
       color = vec4(1.0f); // Set all 4 vector values to 1.0f
   }
   ```

The reason we have passed the value to `vec4` as `1.0f` is so that all the vector values should be set to `1.0f`, which is red, green, blue, and alpha at high intensity. So, it'll be fully on. If you have full red, full green, and full blue, you get white. Thus, our lamp will emit white light.

You might have done an experiment in high school where you get all the different colors of the rainbow on a circle, and if you spin it fast enough, the combined color looks white. It's a pretty cool experiment, and you probably could do that at home. It's worth checking that out, just in general, it's a fun thing to do.

Effects of lighting , Materials and Lightmaps

So, now that we've got our shader files all set up for lighting and lamp we'll move on to our main code in the `main.cpp` file to add an object and light source to our game world.

Modifying the main code to implement a cube and a light source

Now that we have created new shader files for our project we'll next work on our main code and add a colored cube and a light source to our game world. In this section, we'll also take a look at how to reference our newly created shader files in the code. Here, we'll work on the code from the previous chapter and make modifications to it. Perform the following steps to understand the changes made to the code:

1. The first thing that we're going to do, before our `int main()`, is add `glm::vec3 lightPos();`. So, this is going to be the position of the source of light in our world. We'll pass following coordinates to the function `lightpos()`: `1.2f`, `1.0f`, and `2.0f`. The way this works is you have light emitting from a particular location, for example, if you load in a light bulb as a source and you place it at the defined location. The light bulb itself is a light source for our world.

2. Next, we'll go to the section where we've defined our shader. As we've added new shaders to our project, we'll have to reference them in the code.

3. Now that we've got a couple of shaders, what we're going to do is duplicate the `Shader ourShader( );` function present in our code and rename it `lightingShader` and `lampShader`. Obviously, we'll need to update the path mentioned so as to reference our lighting and lamp shader files. Have a look at the following highlighted code:

   ```
   Shader lightingShader( "res/shaders/lighting.vs",
   "res/shaders/lighting.frag" );
   Shader lampShader( "res/shaders/lamp.vs", "res/shaders/lamp.frag"
   );
   ```

4. Next, for the vertices, what we're going to do is remove all the texture coordinates present in our array. As we're not rendering any texture in this code and we only need the x, y, and z coordinates to describe our cube. You can refer to the updated vertices in the `main.cpp` file present in the `colours` folder in the `Chapter04` folder.

5. Then we'll get rid of the `cubePositions []` array as we're going to be rendering a single cube in our world. This will make it easier for us to understand the effect of light on our object.
6. Next, in the code, where we've defined our vertex buffer objects and vertex array objects, we'll make the following modifications to it:

```
    // First, set the container's VAO (and VBO)
       GLuint VBO, boxVAO;
       glGenVertexArrays( 1, &boxVAO );
       glGenBuffers( 1, &VBO );
```

The reason we made this modification is we're going to have a vertex buffer object that we'll just reuse, but for the vertex array object, there'll be a different one for each individual shader and the box.

7. Now, in the position attribute, we'll update the `5 * sizeof()` to `3 * sizeof()` as we no longer have five pieces of information in a row in the vertex array, which were the 3: *x*, *y*, and *z* coordinates and the two texture coordinates. Now, as we are no longer using texture cooordinates we only have *x*, *y*, and *z* coordinates in the array.
8. Next, we'll get rid of the texture coordinate attribute because we're no longer loading textures in our code.
9. Then what we're going to do is duplicate the vertex defining code, vertex binding code, and the position attribute code and paste in below the position attribute code. And in these duplicated lines of code we'll make the following highlighted changes to add the light vertex array object to our main code:

```
    // Then, we set the light's VAO (VBO stays the same. After all, the
    vertices are the same for the light object (also a 3D cube))
    GLuint lightVAO;
    glGenVertexArrays( 1, &lightVAO );
    glBindVertexArray( lightVAO );
     // We only need to bind to the VBO (to link it with
    glVertexAttribPointer), no need to fill it; the VBO's data already
    contains all we need.
     glBindBuffer( GL_ARRAY_BUFFER, VBO );
    // Set the vertex attributes (only position data for the lamp)

    glVertexAttribPointer( 0, 3, GL_FLOAT, GL_FALSE, 3 * sizeof(
    GLfloat ), ( GLvoid * )0 );
    glEnableVertexAttribArray( 0 );
    glBindVertexArray( 0 );
```

Effects of lighting, Materials and Lightmaps

10. The next thing that we're going to do is get rid of the entire create and load texture code.
11. In the previous chapter, we had added the projection matrix within the loop and it was declared every single time the loop ran. Now, because we're getting the field of view using GetZoom we can't place the projection matrix in the loop. So, as a result, we might as well just get the projection matrix code out of the loop and paste it at start of the while loop.

Modifications to the while loop

There's a few things that we need to change inside the while loop, so let's take a look:

1. First of all, we're going to change the background color so we have a darker background so that the lighting that we are trying to implement will have more of effect on our object. So, we'll make the following modifications to the `glClearColor` () function:

    ```
    glClearColor( 0.1f, 0.1f, 0.1f, 1.0f );
    ```

2. What we're going to do next is get rid of all the code from the point where we defined our bind texture code to the point where we define our draw container code and add the fresh code.
3. So, what we're going to do is use the corresponding shader to set the uniform objects and draw the object's code. First of all, what we're going to add `lightingShader.Use();` as we're handling the lighting shader of the box. Then we're going to create a `GLuint` variable, `objectColorLoc`, and to this we'll assign the value of function `glGetUniformLocation` (), which will consists of parameter such as `lightingShader.Program` and `"objectColor"`

> As usual, if you would like to know more details about what we're discussing, you can check out `learnopengl.com` and `open.gl`. They've got some well-written tutorials on there and they've got images to accompany those tutorials, and it's a great way of learning on top of these chapters.

Chapter 4

4. Next, we're going to duplicate the preceding line of code and make the highlighted modifications to it:

   ```
   lightingShader.Use( );
   GLint objectColorLoc = glGetUniformLocation(
   lightingShader.Program, "objectColor" );
   GLint lightColorLoc  = glGetUniformLocation(
   lightingShader.Program, "lightColor" );
   ```

5. Then we're going to add function `glUniform3f()` and to that we're uniforming the object color location. So, we'll pass the parameters as `objectColorLoc` and `1.0f, 0.5f, 0.31f`.

   These are obviously just arbitrary values that we have been determined, and they actually work well. Obviously in your future projects, when you're not following the chapter, you can try experimenting with the values. We'll just duplicate the preceding line of code and make the following highlighted changes to it:

   ```
   glUniform3f( objectColorLoc, 1.0f, 0.5f, 0.31f );
   glUniform3f( lightColorLoc,  1.0f, 0.5f, 1.0f );
   ```

6. And now we're going to create a camera transformation. So, we'll add the view matrix `glm::mat4 view;` to our code and then type `view = camera.GetViewMatrix`.

7. Next, we're going to get the uniform location for the model, view, and projection matrix. So, we're going to type `GLint modelLoc = glGetUniformLocation();`. And in there, we are going to pass `lightingShader.Program` and `model`.

   We'll just duplicate this preceding code a couple of times and make the highlighted changes to it, as follows:

   ```
   // Create camera transformations
   glm::mat4 view;
   view = camera.GetViewMatrix( );

   // Get the uniform locations
   GLint modelLoc = glGetUniformLocation(
   lightingShader.Program,"model");
   GLint viewLoc = glGetUniformLocation(
   lightingShader.Program,"view");
   GLint projLoc = glGetUniformLocation( lightingShader.Program,
   "projection" );
   ```

Effects of lighting, Materials and Lightmaps

8. And now we're going to pass the matrices to the shader. So now, we just need to add `glUniformMatrix4fv();`. And to this function, we'll pass `viewLoc, 1, GL_FALSE, glm::value_ptr()` and for the value pointer function, you just specify our 4x4 view matrix.

9. Duplicate the preceding line of code, as we need to do the same for projection matrix. Check out the following code and the highlighted terms in it:

```
// Pass the matrices to the shader
glUniformMatrix4fv( viewLoc, 1, GL_FALSE, glm::value_ptr( view ) );
glUniformMatrix4fv( projLoc, 1, GL_FALSE, glm::value_ptr( projection ) );
```

10. Now what we're going to do is draw the container using the container's vertex attributes, simple stuff, we've covered this in previous chapters. If you want to review them, feel free. Take a look at the following code:

```
// Draw the container (using container's vertex attributes)
glBindVertexArray( boxVAO );
glm::mat4 model;
glUniformMatrix4fv( modelLoc, 1, GL_FALSE, glm::value_ptr( model ) );
glDrawArrays( GL_TRIANGLES, 0, 36 );
glBindVertexArray( 0 );
```

In the preceding code, we put 36. The reason for this is, as there are a total of 36 vertices, 6 per side, and there are 6 sides to a cube, so we passed 36 in the function `glDrawArrays()`.

11. Next, what we'll do is duplicate the code that we have described in the previous steps and paste it below the preceding code. Then we'll carry out the following highlighted changes for the lamp shader:

```
// Also draw the lamp object, again binding the appropriate shader
lampShader.Use( );
// Get location objects for the matrices on the lamp shader (these
could be different on a different shader)
modelLoc = glGetUniformLocation( lampShader.Program, "model" );
viewLoc = glGetUniformLocation( lampShader.Program, "view" );
projLoc = glGetUniformLocation( lampShader.Program, "projection" );
// Set matrices
glUniformMatrix4fv( viewLoc, 1, GL_FALSE, glm::value_ptr( view ) );
glUniformMatrix4fv( projLoc, 1, GL_FALSE, glm::value_ptr( projection ) );
model = glm::mat4( );
model = glm::translate( model, lightPos );
model = glm::scale( model, glm::vec3( 0.2f ) ); // Make it a
```

```
                smaller cube
                glUniformMatrix4fv( modelLoc, 1, GL_FALSE, glm::value_ptr( model )
                );
                // Draw the light object (using light's vertex attributes)
                glBindVertexArray( lightVAO );
                glDrawArrays( GL_TRIANGLES, 0, 36 );
                glBindVertexArray( 0 );
```

In the preceding code, in `glm::vec3( 0.2f )` we added 0.2f as we wanted to scale it by `0.2f` on every axis. The reason we're scaling it is because we don't want our light source, our lamp, to be the same size as our cube. It's just the way we perceive the world. Generally speaking, a bulb is smaller than most things in the room that we perceive.

12. And now, the only thing we need to do is update `glDeleteVertexArrays()`. We'll update that as follows:

```
                glDeleteVertexArrays( 1, &boxVAO );
                glDeleteVertexArrays( 1, &lightVAO );
                glDeleteBuffers( 1, &VBO );
```

We're now ready to run and see our masterpiece. Check the output on your window:

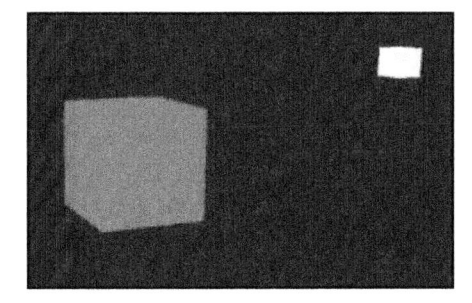

We've got this sort of red-looking box and we've got our white light source. It doesn't look like it's really emitting any light, but this is just the basics. But this is a nice precursor to future sections, and just the future of creating really cool lighting effects.

In the next section, we're going to look at some really cool basic lighting that will make this look a lot better. So, we recommend you do an extra task in the code: figure out where you can change the color of our object and the light emitting object. So, that's it for just basic colors in lighting within modern OpenGL.

Effects of lighting , Materials and Lightmaps

Lighting up objects

In this section, we'll be looking at basics of lighting because so far, if you look at the results from our previous section, which just discussed colors, what we've got is the cube and the light source. At the moment, the entire color in the cube output just looks uniform. It almost doesn't look like a cube, a six-sided shape figure, and the lighting doesn't look very realistic too. Because realistically, in our example, the light source doesn't emit light onto our cube and there is no effect of light and shadow on the cube. So, in this section we'll discuss the basics of lighting and effect on the cube. We'll focus on improving the lighting system so we can have a more realistic effect.

So, let's get started. As usual, we'll begin making modifications to our shader files.

Updating the shaders

Check out the following steps to understand the changes made to the shaders:

1. We're not going to be changing anything in the lamp shader files because we're happy with the actual light that's being emitted.
2. Next, what you want to do is go to your lighting vertex shader and, essentially, change the way our cube perceives the light, and that will make the object look different. So, if you go to our lighting vertex shader, this doesn't require many changes. Take a look at the following highlighted code:

```
#version 330 core
layout (location = 0) in vec3 position;
layout (location = 1) in vec3 normal;

out vec3 Normal;
out vec3 FragPos;

uniform mat4 model;
uniform mat4 view;
uniform mat4 projection;

void main()
{
    gl_Position = projection * view *  model * vec4(position,
    1.0f);
    FragPos = vec3(model * vec4(position, 1.0f));
    Normal = mat3(transpose(inverse(model))) * normal;
}
```

What are normals ?

So, let's first understand what normals are. So, normals are basically a direction. They're perpendicular to a particular surface:

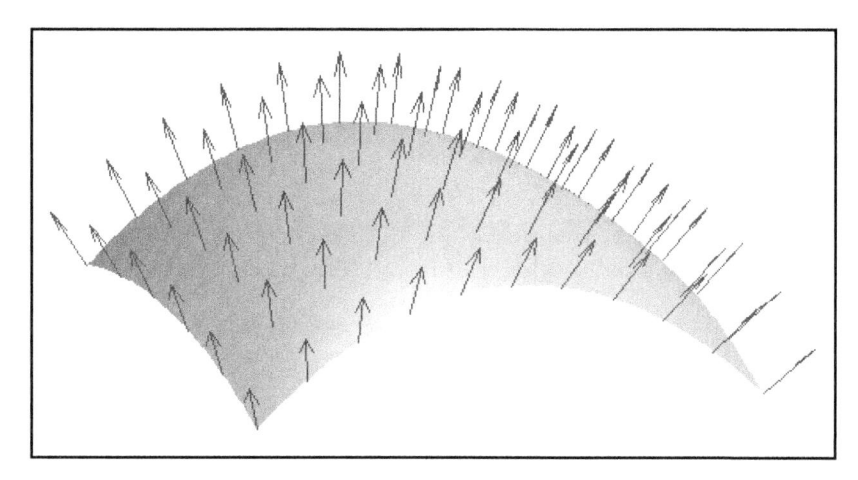

So, as you can see in the preceding diagram, the normals are at 90 degrees to the surface, and this is useful when calculating lighting because it determines the way light bounces off the surface, the way the surface reacts to light, and as a result, it looks a certain way. A powerful technique is to change the direction of the normals, which you can do (we'll be covering that in later sections) and that allows you to change the way that the light reacts to it, which makes the object look different. And what we can even do is have, let's say, a flat object, or a relatively flat object with a very low polygon count and by changing the normals, we can add the illusion of depth to it. That's the reason why when you play a game sometimes and you see some sort of object, especially when it's on a wall, it's relatively flat, but it looks like it has a bit of depth to it. If you're quite far away from it, it looks like it's got depth. When you go close, and especially when you look at it from an angle, it doesn't have depth anymore, or it has very little depth. And that's the limitation of this system. Obviously, if you want to get around that, you need to use some sort of tessellation technique that actually has real geometry. That's obviously a lot more expensive in terms of processing power. This is a lot cheaper in terms of processing power, so this is really preferred in the gaming industry, simply because you're not just drawing one sort of simple shape. You're drawing a whole heap of polygons, which this technique will allow you to reserve some processing power.

Effects of lighting , Materials and Lightmaps

Updating the lighting.frag shader

Let's follow the below mentioned steps:

1. So now that we've done this, we go to the lighting fragment shader and make the following highlighted changes to it:

   ```
   #version 330 core
   out vec4 color;
   in vec3 FragPos;
   in vec3 Normal;
   ```

   In the preceding code, we added `FragPos`, as those are going to be the fragment positions that we were sending out from the vertex shader.

2. Then we created uniform vector variables as follow:

   ```
   uniform vec3 lightPos;
   uniform vec3 viewPos;
   uniform vec3 lightColor;
   uniform vec3 objectColor;
   ```

   In the preceding code, we added `lightPos` as we needed a vector for the light position because we are factoring the light position and the lighting will vary depending on what part of the surface you're looking at.

And in our main function there are three types of lighting techniques that we'll be using as shading techniques, and they will be ambient, diffuse, and specular. We'll discuss them in detail and also understand how to define them in our code.

Ambient lighting

The first one, which is ambient lighting, is just like the general lighting that's in a scene. It's not like the light from the sun, but it's general light that is always bouncing around the room. It doesn't have a particular origin or a position or direction. So that allows it to provide some basic sort of color, some basic property to your object. On top of that, you add diffuse lighting and specular lighting to make the object a unique and interesting object to make it look more like what it would in the real world.

We'll begin by adding `float ambientStrength`, and to that we will add value of `0.1f`. Feel free to change that value and see what happens, see the limitations of the variables as well. And then we're going to add `vec3` for the ambient lighting. That variable is going to equal to `ambientStrength * lightColor`:

```
void main()
{
 // Ambient
 float ambientStrength = 0.1f;
 vec3 ambient = ambientStrength * lightColor;
```

Diffuse lighting

Now we're going to do diffuse lighting. Diffuse lighting takes into account the direction and the normal of the light. For example, imagine our cube, the corner which is nearer to the light source will be brighter compared to the corner that is furthest away. Essentially, what is diffuse lighting? It adjusts the actual position and the angle as well. It's to do with the angle as well, so if you were to have a light source at 90 degrees, that would emit more light than, let's say, one at 5 degrees, and 90 degrees would be shinier. That's essentially what diffuse is. You don't generally just have ambient, diffuse, or specular lighting. You have all three combined, at different intensities and different strengths, and that allows you to create a realistic effect called combined lighting, and this effect is very often known as Phong shading. You can read about it on the internet. Take a look at the following code for diffuse light:

```
// Diffuse
 vec3 norm = normalize(Normal);
 vec3 lightDir = normalize(lightPos - FragPos);
 float diff = max(dot(norm, lightDir), 0.0);
 vec3 diffuse = diff * lightColor;
```

In the preceding code, we added `lightPos - FragPos`. The difference between these will tell you the direction in which the light is pointing. At the end of code we're always going to be factoring in the `lightColor` because at the end of the day, if we have a white light shining on something, we don't want it to be blue or red. It has to be what the light is. Obviously, it will vary depending on the actual material that is applied and the sort of properties of that object, but the actual light itself should be a light color.

Now that we've done diffuse lighting, we can go on to specular lighting.

Effects of lighting, Materials and Lightmaps

Specular lighting

To talk about specular lighting, imagine a snooker ball or a pool ball, for example, which has a little circle of light shining on it, it's always that little shiny light on an object. Let's take a look at the code:

```
// Specular
float specularStrength = 0.5f;
vec3 viewDir = normalize(viewPos - FragPos);
vec3 reflectDir = reflect(-lightDir, norm);
float spec = pow(max(dot(viewDir, reflectDir), 0.0), 32);
vec3 specular = specularStrength * spec * lightColor;

vec3 result = (ambient + diffuse + specular) * objectColor;
color = vec4(result, 1.0f);
}
```

Now that we're done updating the shader files, we need to make a minor change in our `Camera.h` file.

Minor change in Camera.h

In the `Camera.h` file, we don't have any sort of method to get the position of the camera. So, what we'll do is, below `glfloat GetZoom()`, we'll add the `glm::vec3 GetPosition()` method and its simply going to return the position. Have a look at the following code:

```
glm::vec3 GetPosition ()
{
    return this ->position
}
```

Making changes to the main code

Now we just need to go to our `main.cpp` file and make modifications to our code. Take a look at the following steps:

1. In there, the first thing that we need to modify is this vertices array. At the moment, we have x, y, and z values for each of the vertices, and what we also need to include is the normal. You can refer to the updated vertices in the `main.cpp` file present in the `Basic Lighting` folder. For reference, just take a look at the vertices of one side of cube:

   ```
   //Position            //Normal
   ```

Chapter 4

```
-0.5f, -0.5f, -0.5f,   0.0f, 0.0f, -1.0f,
 0.5f, -0.5f, -0.5f,   0.0f, 0.0f, -1.0f,
 0.5f,  0.5f, -0.5f,   0.0f, 0.0f, -1.0f,
 0.5f,  0.5f, -0.5f,   0.0f, 0.0f, -1.0f,
-0.5f,  0.5f, -0.5f,   0.0f, 0.0f, -1.0f,
-0.5f, -0.5f, -0.5f,   0.0f, 0.0f, -1.0f,
```

The three extra values that we have got in the preceding array are the direction of the normals. The normals will stay the same for every single face.

> Extra task: Try figuring out which face each one of these normals applies to, and what is the direction once you've rendered it. Modify them, see what happens. Change some of these values, but keep some of them the same. See what happens.

2. Once we've got all of that sorted, we just need to change a few things where we have defined our `VBO` and `boxVAO`. Wherever we have mentioned `boxVAO` we'll replace it with `containerVAO`:

   ```
   GLuint VBO, containerVAO;
   glGenVertexArrays( 1, &containerVAO );
   glGenBuffers( 1, &VBO );

   glBindBuffer( GL_ARRAY_BUFFER, VBO );
   glBufferData( GL_ARRAY_BUFFER, sizeof( vertices ), vertices,
   GL_STATIC_DRAW );

   glBindVertexArray( containerVAO );
   ```

3. In the position attribute we will make the following highlighted changes, and similarly, we'll also create our normal attribute. Take a look at the following highlighted code:

   ```
   // Position attribute
     glVertexAttribPointer( 0, 3, GL_FLOAT, GL_FALSE, 6 * sizeof(
   GLfloat ), ( GLvoid * )0 );
     glEnableVertexAttribArray( 0 );

   // Normal attribute
     glVertexAttribPointer( 1, 3, GL_FLOAT, GL_FALSE, 6 * sizeof(
   GLfloat ), ( GLvoid * )( 3 * sizeof( GLfloat ) ) );
     glEnableVertexAttribArray( 1 );
     glBindVertexArray( 0 );
   ```

Effects of lighting, Materials and Lightmaps

As we've got six different pieces of value on each row of the vertices array, which is the reason why we updated 6 in our code. You will updated the similar value of 6 in the `lightVAO` position attribute too.

4. Where we are defining our lighting shader in the code, we're using the object color location and the light color location. Now, what we also need to do is add the lighting position location and assign that to our shader program, and also add the view position location. So, what we're going to do is duplicate the whole `GLint lightColorLoc` code twice and make the following updates to add the light position location and the view position location. We need to do a similar thing for `gluniform3f();` too. Take a look at the following highlighted code:

```
lightingShader.Use( );
  GLint objectColorLoc = glGetUniformLocation(
lightingShader.Program, "objectColor" );
  GLint lightColorLoc = glGetUniformLocation(
lightingShader.Program, "lightColor" );
  GLint lightPosLoc = glGetUniformLocation( lightingShader.Program,
"lightPos" );
  GLint viewPosLoc = glGetUniformLocation( lightingShader.Program,
"viewPos" );
  glUniform3f( objectColorLoc, 1.0f, 0.5f, 0.31f );
  glUniform3f( lightColorLoc, 1.0f, 1.0f, 1.0f );
  glUniform3f( lightPosLoc, lightPos.x, lightPos.y, lightPos.z );
  glUniform3f( viewPosLoc, camera.GetPosition( ).x,
camera.GetPosition( ).y, camera.GetPosition( ).z )
```

Once we have got all of this updated, we'll leave rest of the code as it. As we don't have to make any modifications to it.

We should actually be ready to run the code, but remember what it looked like in the previous section. The output that you got on your screen should look some what similar to this:

As you may have noticed in the preceding image, the top-left side, by the top-left corner, looks a little brighter than the bottom left, and that's because that's where the light source is. And it's definitely evident on the other sides of the cube and on the top. Just take a look at the top compared to other sides. Those sides are darker as they have hardly any light on their surfaces. You can check that out in the following screenshot:

It's just, it's a lot more realistic than it was before. You'll also notice as you move across it, you will get to see the beautiful dynamic shading on our cube.

So what we're going to do now is go to the lighting fragment shader and change the `specularStrength` to `2.0f`. Just modify this stuff up, and just observe the output that will have, take a look at the following screenshot:

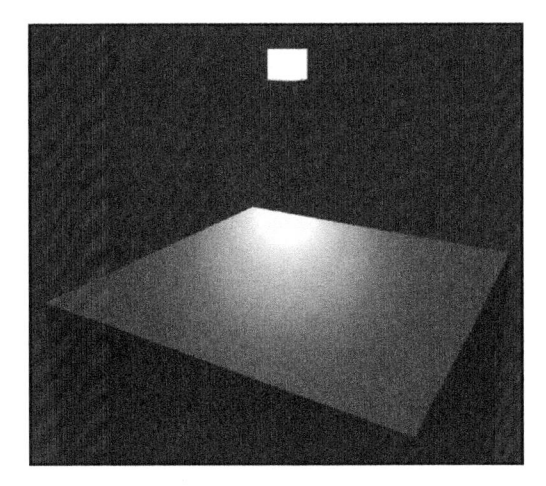

Effects of lighting , Materials and Lightmaps

You can already see the sort of impact that change of value in the code had on the intensity of light. Look at that shine. That's the sort of shine that you get on a pool ball. Try experimenting with the value. If you change the value of `ambientStrength` to `0.5f` you'll see a brighter cube:

This is almost looking more like a uniform color now, but it looks quite cool as well. Try experimenting by changing the values in your shader files and the main code.

One last thing that we'll try doing is to move the light position so you can actually sort of see what effect it has on our object. So, in our main code, at the start of while loop, we'll add `lightPos.x -= 0.01f`, and we're going to do the same for the z position:

```
lightPos.x -= 0.01f
lightPos.z -= 0.01f
```

We're not going to modify the y position because we sort of only want the light source to move along the horizon. You could make it move along the y axis as well; we recommend you do that. Try and make a circle around it. Save the changes and run the code. You'll observe the following output on your screen:

As you can see, we've got a light and as it's getting further away, the top side is getting dark because it's at a really obscure angle. As it's getting further and further away, you will observe that the top side gets darker and darker:

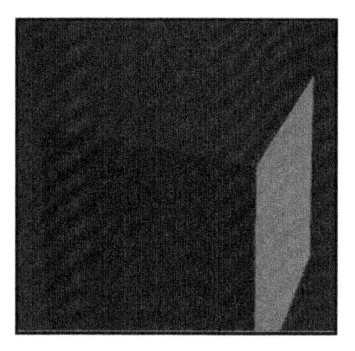

As an extra task, we recommend trying to move the light as far as you can and observe the effect. It would be fantastic if you could get it to rotate around the object itself and try adding multiple lights. That will create an awesome effect.

Materials

We're going to discuss materials in this section. So, let's first understand what a material is and why would you use it. In the real world, you have objects that are made out of different materials. You have objects that are made out of metals, wood, plastic, and other stuff. As a result, these materials, these objects, react differently to light depending on what they're made out of. Generally speaking, something that's made out of metal will be shinier than something that's made out of wood. Wood generally isn't shiny. Obviously, it is if you apply some sort of varnish to it, but again, that would be an additional layer to the object that's not wood. It'd be something more than wood that is applied on top of it that provides some sort of shine to it. You have glossy materials, and you have some more matte materials. Simply put, materials in OpenGL will allow us to create objects that react differently to light, and as a result, create more realistic and varied effects in our game or application. And that's why you would use it, to get a more varied and realistic representation of the objects you are trying to create.

Effects of lighting, Materials and Lightmaps

So, let's get started...

As few prerequisites. This section is using the source code from the previous section, which was covering basic lighting. If you haven't got the code for that, feel free to check out the GitHub link in the preface for the code files. The other thing we want to mention is that these chapters are based on the work of learnopengl.com and open.gl. They're using a fantastic illustrations to explain what we're doing. Also, feel free to check out their pages because they've got some great information. They go into really great depth into the code that we have discussed in all the chapters. So, it's just a great way of enhancing the knowledge you already know.

What we're going to do in this section is make the cube cycle through various different materials. We'll begin by updating the shader files.

Updating shader files for Materials

Take a look at the following steps

1. We won't make any changes to the vertex shader, that is, `lighting.vs`.
2. Next, we'll move onto the lighting fragment shader and in here, right at the top, we're going to create a data type `struct` called `Material`. In there, we're going to have three varibles `vec3`, which are going to be the `ambient`, the `diffuse`, the `specular`, and the `shininess` float, so we can easily change the intensity of the specular light. Take a look at the following code:

   ```
   struct Material
   {
        vec3 ambient;
        vec3 diffuse;
        vec3 specular;
        float shininess;
   };
   ```

3. Next, we're going to create a datatype struct for Light. This is going to have a `vec3` of position and it's going to have three more `vec3` for ambient, diffuse, and specular:

   ```
   struct Light
   {
        vec3 position;

        vec3 ambient;
        vec3 diffuse;
   ```

```
    vec3 specular;
};
```

> If you want to know a bit more about what ambient, diffuse, and specular are, feel free to check out the previous the sections. Or, feel free to go to learnopengl.com and open.gl. These sites provide a lot of information.

4. Then, we'll get rid of the `lightPos` because we have it within the preceding struct. We don't want `objectColor`, and also we don't want `lightColor` as well, because again, we've got it all within our struct. Then we'll add `uniform Material material` and we also add `uniform Light light`:

```
uniform vec3 viewPos;
uniform Material material;
uniform Light light;
```

5. And now, in `void main()`, what are we going to do? For the ambient light, we'll get rid of the `ambientStrength` and we'll modify it as `Vec3 ambient = light.ambient * material.ambient`.

6. And for the diffuse light, `vec3 lightDir`, we need to change that up a bit. Take a look at the highlighted terms:

```
vec3 lightDir = normalize(light.position - FragPos);
```

7. And for the final diffuse calculation, all we need to do is change it up slightly. We need to add `light.diffuse` multiplied by `diff`, which was calculated here in the float variable, and `diff` multiplied by `material.diffuse`. We are factoring in material in every single part of our lighting, our shading, simply because that's what's important. That's the way that our actual object will look, or that part of the object, because we have different materials applied.

8. In specular, we can get rid of `specularStrength` because we've got that in the previous code. Then we'll update `float spec` for the shininess; we'll add `material.shininess`. For `vec3 specular`, we are changing that up slightly. We're going to add `light.specular * (spec * material.specular)`. And for the result, we'll modify that as highlighted in the following code:

```
void main()
{
 // Ambient
 vec3 ambient = light.ambient * material.ambient;

 // Diffuse
 vec3 norm = normalize(Normal);
```

Effects of lighting , Materials and Lightmaps

```
    vec3 lightDir = normalize(light.position - FragPos);
    float diff = max(dot(norm, lightDir), 0.0);
    vec3 diffuse = light.diffuse * (diff * material.diffuse);

    // Specular
    vec3 viewDir = normalize(viewPos - FragPos);
    vec3 reflectDir = reflect(-lightDir, norm);
    float spec = pow(max(dot(viewDir, reflectDir), 0.0),
material.shininess);
    vec3 specular = light.specular * (spec * material.specular);

    vec3 result = ambient + diffuse + specular;
    color = vec4(result, 1.0f);
}
```

Save these changes, and now we are done updating the fragment shader.

Making changes to the main code to add materials to our object

Follow the below mentioned steps to add materials to our object and observe the effects of light on it:

1. If you go to `main.cpp`, what you want to do is actually go straight to the while loop, because everything outside of that should is fine and doesn't need any modification.
2. So, in lines of code below `lightingShader.Use();`, we'll get rid of `objectColorLoc` and `lightColorLoc`. We want `lightPosLoc`, but a parameter in it needs to be changed to `light.position` because we've updated that in our fragment shader.
3. In `gluniform3f` you can get rid of `objectColorLoc` and `lightColorLoc`.

4. Now we need to also set the light's properties. For that, we'll add `glm::vec3 lightColor;` and we'll add `lightColor.r = sin();`, and for `sin()`, this is where we're going to have some framework-specific code. We're just going to be pass `glfwGetTime()`, which just gets the amount of time that has passed since GLFW was initialized. We'll just multiply `glfwGetTime()` by `2.0f`. We'll duplicate this line of code, paste it below, and make the following highlighted modification to it:

```
// Set lights properties
glm::vec3 lightColor;
lightColor.r = sin( glfwGetTime( ) * 2.0f );
lightColor.g = sin( glfwGetTime( ) * 0.7f );
lightColor.b = sin( glfwGetTime( ) * 1.3f );
```

5. So now that we've set the light's properties, we need to actually do the diffuse color and the ambient color. So, we're going to add `glm::vec3 diffuseColor = lightColor * glm::vec3();`. And for `ver3()`, we're just going to provide a value of `0.5f`. This is just going to decrease the influence of the diffuse color.

6. Next, we're going to add `glm::vec3 ambientColor = diffuseColor * glm::vec3();` and over here, `vec3` is going to be `0.2f`, as this is just a low-intensity one. So try some experimenting by modifying these values and see what you come up.

7. Then, what we need to add is `glUniform3f()` function and to that, we'll pass `glGetUniformLocation()` function and for this function now we're going to specify `lightingShader.Program` and `"light.ambient"`. Then we're going to pass `ambientColor.r` and similarly, we'll pass `ambientColor.g` and `ambientColor.b`.

8. Next, what we'll do is just duplicate the previously described code and make the following highlighted changes to it:

```
glm::vec3 diffuseColor = lightColor * glm::vec3( 0.5f ); // Decrease the influence
glm::vec3 ambientColor = diffuseColor * glm::vec3( 0.2f ); // Low influence
glUniform3f( glGetUniformLocation( lightingShader.Program, "light.ambient" ), ambientColor.r, ambientColor.g, ambientColor.b );
glUniform3f( glGetUniformLocation( lightingShader.Program, "light.diffuse" ), diffuseColor.r, diffuseColor.g, diffuseColor.b);
glUniform3f( glGetUniformLocation( lightingShader.Program, "light.specular" ), 1.0f, 1.0f, 1.0f );
```

Effects of lighting, Materials and Lightmaps

9. Now we're going to set the material properties, and to do that, we're going to do the ambient, the diffuse, the specular, and the shininess of the material. So, you want to add `glUniform3f();` and to that, we'll pass `glGetUniformLocation()`, and to this function, we'll specify `lightingShader.Program` and the selected `material.ambient`. Then we'll pass some values. We're going to just put some explicit values as `1.0f, 0.5f,` and `0.31f`.

10. Just copy and paste the previous code several times and make the following modifications as highlighted in the following code:

```
// Set material properties
glUniform3f( glGetUniformLocation( lightingShader.Program, "material.ambient" ), 1.0f, 0.5f, 0.31f );
glUniform3f( glGetUniformLocation( lightingShader.Program, "material.diffuse"), 1.0f, 0.5f, 0.31f );
glUniform3f (glGetUniformLocation( lightingShader.Program, "material.specular" ), 0.5f, 0.5f, 0.5f ); // Specular doesn't have full effect on this object's material
glUniform1f (glGetUniformLocation( lightingShader.Program, "material.shininess" ), 32.0f );
```

In the preceding code, while defining shininess we have added just 1 float value in `glUniform1f()` because the shininess wasn't a vector or an array, or anything like that.

Now we are all set with the code. So let's run this code and check the output that we get on our screen. You might get a similar output on your window:

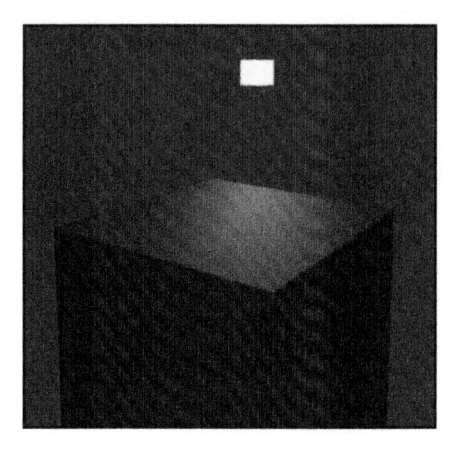

You'll observe a color changing cube on your screen. It looks exactly the way we want, just beautiful. Try moving the light and observe the shadow effect on the surface of the cube:

So that it's for using materials in OpenGL to add effects to our object.

Lightmaps

Let's discuss lightmaps in this section. But first, let's try to understand what a lighting map is. Well, in the real world, if you have, let's say, a crate that is partly metal and partly wood, similar to the following screenshot:

Effects of lighting , Materials and Lightmaps

The wooden parts of it will react differently to the light compared to the metal parts. It might sound obvious, but OpenGL (or any other sort of 3D graphics API) doesn't have a concept of wood or metal or plastic, or anything else and as a result, we need to program that in. We need to use other techniques to help illustrate that visually as the wood should be less shiny than the metal parts of the crate. If you search on lighting maps, you'll get a bunch of information. You can create them in various tools. You can use Maya or Photoshop to create them. So, without further ado, let's get down to the coding.

Making modifications to shader files

Follow the below mentioned steps:

1. So, what you want to do is go to the lighting vertex shader. We need to make a few modifications to this because we removed the ability to apply textures, and we didn't do that in the last couple of sections. So, we need to add that again. Take a look at the following modification to understand the changes made to the code:

```
#version 330 core
layout (location = 0) in vec3 position;
layout (location = 1) in vec3 normal;
layout (location = 2) in vec2 texCoords;

out vec3 Normal;
out vec3 FragPos;
out vec2 TexCoords;

uniform mat4 model;
uniform mat4 view;
uniform mat4 projection;

void main()
{
    gl_Position = projection * view * model * vec4(position, 1.0f);
    FragPos = vec3(model * vec4(position, 1.0f));
    Normal = mat3(transpose(inverse(model))) * normal;
    TexCoords = texCoords;
}
```

Save these changes, and now we need to do a modification to the fragment shader.

Chapter 4

2. In `lighting.frag`, we'll make the following changes to the code: We'll get rid of all the code from the struct material and add fresh code to it. We'll add `sampler2D diffuse` and `sampler2D specular`, and this is that specular lightmap that had the light part and the dark part on it. Then we'll add `float shininess`. Shininess is always important:

   ```
   struct Material
   {
       sampler2D diffuse;
       sampler2D specular;
       float shininess;
   };
   ```

3. For the input, we also need the texture coordinate. So we'll add `in vec2 TexCoords`:

   ```
   struct Light
   {
       vec3 position;

       vec3 ambient;
       vec3 diffuse;
       vec3 specular;
   };

   in vec3 FragPos;
   in vec3 Normal;
   in vec2 TexCoords;

   out vec4 color;

   uniform vec3 viewPos;
   uniform Material material;
   uniform Light light;
   ```

4. Now, `void main ()` in vec3 ambient needs to change slightly because we are using a texture. So, what we need to do is just get rid of `material.ambient` and add `vec3()` and inside that, we want to specify `texture()`. Inside this method, we're going to pass `material.diffuse` and `TexCoords`.

[139]

5. Now, for the diffuse light in the final calculation, (`diff * material.diffuse`) needs to change slightly, as we are using textures now. So, what we're going to do is just get rid of the preceding term and add `light.diffuse * diff * vec3()`. To that, we'll pass `texture()`, and in that, we'll specify `material.diffuse` and `TexCoords`. The rest all is good. Let's go down to specular now. In the final step, we just need to change it in a similar way to the previous one because we are using a texture now. Take a look at the following code to understand the description:

```
void main()
{
    // Ambient
    vec3 ambient = light.ambient * vec3(texture(material.diffuse, TexCoords));

    // Diffuse
    vec3 norm = normalize(Normal);
    vec3 lightDir = normalize(light.position - FragPos);
    float diff = max(dot(norm, lightDir), 0.0);
    vec3 diffuse = light.diffuse * diff * vec3(texture(material.diffuse, TexCoords));

    // Specular
    vec3 viewDir = normalize(viewPos - FragPos);
    vec3 reflectDir = reflect(-lightDir, norm);
    float spec = pow(max(dot(viewDir, reflectDir), 0.0), material.shininess);
    vec3 specular = light.specular * spec * vec3(texture(material.specular, TexCoords));

    color = vec4(ambient + diffuse + specular, 1.0f);
}
```

So, we're all done with the shaders now. We can actually get to main.cpp.

Changes to the main code to implement lightmaps

Let's follow the below mentioned steps to implement the lightmaps:

1. In the main code, the first thing you'll need to change is the vertices, because at the moment we've got position and we've got the normals as well. We also need to specify the texture coordinates because we now are using a texture. You can refer to the updated vertices in the `main.cpp` file inside the `Lighting Maps` folder. Copy and paste the updated vertices to our main code.

2. Next, go to the location where we're binding the vertex and creating the vertex pointers. As we have added a texture system to our code, we need to modify the vertex pointer and the normal attribute slightly. As we've got eight pieces of information in our vertices array, we'll replace the 6 with 8. We also need to duplicate the Normal attribute code, paste it, and modify it for the texture attribute. Take a look at the following code to understand the modifications made:

   ```
   glBindVertexArray( containerVAO );
   glVertexAttribPointer( 0, 3, GL_FLOAT, GL_FALSE, 8 * sizeof( GLfloat ), ( GLvoid * )0 );
   glEnableVertexAttribArray( 0 );
   glVertexAttribPointer( 1, 3, GL_FLOAT, GL_FALSE, 8 * sizeof( GLfloat ), ( GLvoid * )( 3 * sizeof( GLfloat ) ) );
   glEnableVertexAttribArray( 1 );
   glVertexAttribPointer( 2, 2, GL_FLOAT, GL_FALSE, 8 * sizeof( GLfloat ), ( GLvoid * )( 6 * sizeof( GLfloat ) ) );
   glEnableVertexAttribArray( 2 );
   ```

3. Now let's take a look at the lighting array. In the position attribute, change the 6 to 8 for a similar reason as mentioned in the previous code.

4. You don't have to necessarily do this before we do the projection, but we are going to. We're just going to load the textures before we define our projection matrix. We're going to create the diffuse and the specular maps as well, since you just load in two different textures. We've covered this before. So, we'll add `GLuint`, `diffuseMap`, and `specularMap`. Then we're adding `glGenTextures();`. And to that, we'll pass the parameters for the `size` as 1, and for the `pointer` we're going to add `&diffuseMap` and copy and paste this code to save some time. We'll make the following changes to the copied code:

   ```
   // Load textures
   GLuint diffuseMap, specularMap;
   ```

Effects of lighting, Materials and Lightmaps

```
        glGenTextures( 1, &diffuseMap );
        glGenTextures( 1, &specularMap );
```

5. Now we need to create an int for the texture width and height.
6. Then we are going to add `unsigned char *image`. This is essentially going to be the data of our image, because if you ever try to open up an image in some sort of text editor, you just get a bunch of characters. This is essentially what this is going to be storing:

    ```
    int textureWidth, textureHeight;
    unsigned char *image;
    ```

7. So, now we're going to add the diffuse map. We'll begin by adding `image = SOIL_LOAD_IMAGE();`. To this, first of all, we need to specify the file path of the image, which is `res/images/container2.png`. For the width and the height parameters, we just specify the `&textureWidth` and `&textureHeight` that we created before, because this is passing it in a reference, and it'll actually modify the original variable right here. For channels, put 0. For `force_channels`, just put `SOIL_LOAD_RGB`.

8. And in the next line, we need to add `glBindTexture();`. The parameter we'll pass for the target is just `GL_TEXTURE_2D` and for the texture, we just specify `diffuseMap`, because that's the one we're using at the moment.

9. Now, on the next line we need to add `glTexImage2D();`. The parameter we'll pass for the target is just `GL_TEXTURE_2D`. For the level, put 0. For the internal format, this is just `Gl_RGB` because it's got no alpha. For the width, you just put `textureWidth` then `textureHeight`. For the border, put 0. For the format, put `GL_RGB`. For the type, we're going to put `GL_UNSIGNED_BYTE`. For the `pixels`, just specify the image data, which is `image`.

10. Next, we're just going to generate the mipmap, so add `glGenerateMipmap();`, and to that, we're going to pass `GL_TEXTURE_2D`.

11. Then add `SOIL_free_image_data()`. Here, we'll just specify the image that we want to free.

12. Next, we just need to specify the texture parameters in terms of the wrapping and the filtering. So, we'll add `glTextParameteri();`. For this, we'll pass the target parameter as `GL_TEXTURE_2D`. For the `name`, for what we're modifying, it is the wrap for now, so pass `GL_TEXTURE_WRAP_S` a and then pass `GL_REPEAT`.

13. Let's just duplicate this code and paste it below. Check out the following code to understand the modifications we need to make:

    ```
    // Diffuse map
    image = SOIL_load_image( "res/images/container2.png",
    ```

```
    &textureWidth, &textureHeight, 0, SOIL_LOAD_RGB );
    glBindTexture( GL_TEXTURE_2D, diffuseMap );
    glTexImage2D( GL_TEXTURE_2D, 0, GL_RGB, textureWidth,
textureHeight, 0, GL_RGB, GL_UNSIGNED_BYTE, image );
    glGenerateMipmap( GL_TEXTURE_2D );
    SOIL_free_image_data( image );
    glTexParameteri( GL_TEXTURE_2D, GL_TEXTURE_WRAP_S, GL_REPEAT );
    glTexParameteri( GL_TEXTURE_2D, GL_TEXTURE_WRAP_T, GL_REPEAT );
    glTexParameteri( GL_TEXTURE_2D, GL_TEXTURE_MIN_FILTER,
GL_LINEAR_MIPMAP_LINEAR );
    glTexParameteri( GL_TEXTURE_2D, GL_TEXTURE_MAG_FILTER,
GL_NEAREST_MIPMAP_NEAREST );
```

14. And now we're done with defining the diffuse map. What we're going to do next is actually just duplicate all this code for the specular map because it'll be a lot easier and because a lot of it's going to stay the same. Take look at the following highlighted terms to understand the changes:

```
// Specular map
    image = SOIL_load_image( "res/images/container2_specular.png",
    &textureWidth, &textureHeight, 0, SOIL_LOAD_RGB );
    glBindTexture( GL_TEXTURE_2D, specularMap );
    glTexImage2D( GL_TEXTURE_2D, 0, GL_RGB, textureWidth,
textureHeight, 0, GL_RGB, GL_UNSIGNED_BYTE, image );
    glGenerateMipmap( GL_TEXTURE_2D );
    SOIL_free_image_data( image );
    glTexParameteri( GL_TEXTURE_2D, GL_TEXTURE_WRAP_S, GL_REPEAT );
    glTexParameteri( GL_TEXTURE_2D, GL_TEXTURE_WRAP_T, GL_REPEAT );
    glTexParameteri( GL_TEXTURE_2D, GL_TEXTURE_MIN_FILTER,
GL_LINEAR_MIPMAP_LINEAR );
    glTexParameteri( GL_TEXTURE_2D, GL_TEXTURE_MAG_FILTER,
GL_NEAREST_MIPMAP_NEAREST );
    glBindTexture( GL_TEXTURE_2D, 0 );
```

In the preceding code, at the end we unbound texture by defining glBindTexture(GL_TEXTURE_2D, 0);.

15. And now, we just need to set the texture units for the lighting shader. So, we're going to add lightingShader.Use(); and on the next line we are going to add glUniform1i, and we're going to specify glGetUniformLocation lightingShader.Program. And we just need to pass material.diffuse and o This is all stuff that we did in the shader, so feel free to look at that again if you just need a quick reminder. We're all good now:

```
// Set texture units
    lightingShader.Use( );
```

Effects of lighting, Materials and Lightmaps

```
glUniform1i( glGetUniformLocation( lightingShader.Program,
"material.diffuse" ), 0 );
glUniform1i( glGetUniformLocation( lightingShader.Program,
"material.specular" ), 1 );
```

Modifying while loop

We can actually start coding stuff within the while loop:

1. We're going to set the light's properties. So, what we're going to do is just get rid of all of the `lightColor` code and we're going to add `glUniform3f();`. To that, we'll pass `glGetUniformLocation()`, and to this, we'll specify `lightingShader.Program` and we just need to specify the first aspect that we're modifying, which is `light.ambient`, and we're just going to put some hardcoded values in here: `0.2f, 0.2f,` and `0.2f`.

2. Let's duplicate this so we've got three instances of it and make following modifications to it:

   ```
   // Set lights properties
   glUniform3f( glGetUniformLocation( lightingShader.Program,
   "light.ambient" ), 0.2f, 0.2f, 0.2f );
   glUniform3f( glGetUniformLocation( lightingShader.Program,
   "light.diffuse" ), 0.5f, 0.5f, 0.5f );
   glUniform3f( glGetUniformLocation( lightingShader.Program,
   "light.specular" ), 1.0f, 1.0f, 1.0f );
   ```

3. So now, let's set the material properties as follows:

   ```
   // Set material properties
   glUniform1f( glGetUniformLocation( lightingShader.Program,
   "material.shininess"), 32.0f );
   ```

4. Now we need to actually activate our textures, and bind them. So below `glUniformMatrix4fv();` we'll add following code:

   ```
   // Bind diffuse map
       glActiveTexture( GL_TEXTURE0 );
       glBindTexture( GL_TEXTURE_2D, diffuseMap );
   ```

5. And you can copy and paste this for the binding of the specular texture map:

   ```
   // Bind specular map
       glActiveTexture( GL_TEXTURE1 );
       glBindTexture( GL_TEXTURE_2D, specularMap );
   ```

Chapter 4

And now we are now ready to run it. You might observe the following output on your screen:

Move around the cube; you will see that as we're moving, the lighting affects the shape in a different way because when we were looking at it head on, there wasn't much of a shine. There's a bit towards the top right; that's when we're moving. It's realistically affecting our object. As you move the light around you can see that only the metal part of it is shining:

[145]

Effects of lighting , Materials and Lightmaps

Obviously, it depends on what sort of angle you're looking at the object from, because that's how it is in real life. So, that's it for lighting maps.

Summary

In this chapter, we learned to apply colors to our objects and create a light source such as a lamp in our game world. We then looked at the effects of light on the materials. We also understood the different types of lighting techniques: ambient, diffused, specular lighting. We explored the various materials and observed the effects of light on the materials. We concluded by learning about lightmaps in this chapter.

In the next chapter, we'll discuss about the different sources of light such as directional light, point light and spot light and how to combine those in our game world.

5
Types of light sources and combining of lights

In this chapter, we'll discuss the various types of lighting effects, such as diffuse light, ambient light, and specular light. You'll also explore the different type of light sources, such as directional light, point light, and spot light. We'll also discuss how to combine these different types of light sources for your game world.

In this chapter we'll cover the following topics:

- Implementing different light sources, such as directional, point, and spot light
- Understanding the different effects of lights, such as diffused, ambient, and specular
- How to combine different effects of light and the sources in your game world

Let's get started.

> You can refer to all the code files for this chapter in the `Chapter05` folder on GitHub. The GitHub link can be found in the preface of the book.

Directional light

In this section, we're going to talk about a directional light. We are advancing quite a bit now into the different lighting mechanics that you can use in OpenGL. We've looked at lighting maps, to be able to shine a light and have it affect an object differently depending on what sort of material a particular object or a particular part of the object is.

Directional lights

We've looked at other basic material and basic lighting, but there are a few main types of lights that you can use in your game, such as directional lights, point lights, and spotlights. We'll be covering point lights and spotlights in later sections; but directional lights are the most basic version of lights in 3D graphics, in general:

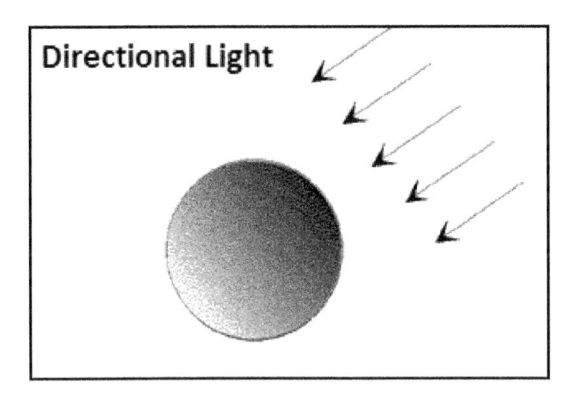

So, as you can see in the preceding diagram, there are arrows coming from some sort of light source. A directional light doesn't have an origin, or more precisely, a position, because the light source is infinitely far away.

So, for example, you had five cubes. Irrespective of what material they are, let's just assume they were all the same and they were rotated in the same way, but were positioned all over the place. So, let's say each one of them was (we don't really have a concept of distance in miles or kilometers in our engine) 100 miles away from each other and in any direction. The actual light and the directional light would affect each individual box object in the same way because the directional light has no starting position. You can't get any closer to the light source; you might think that if you move in the light's direction, you'll get closer to the light source. Technically, you could say that's true. But if it has no original location and no original position, and it's infinitely far away, it's still going to be infinitely far away. So that's what a directional light is.

A directional light is sort of just a general light you have in the scene, and then you use spotlights and point lights to enhance your scene to create more specific stuff. So, let's consider this example. If you have a game that's set on flat ground or some island, then the directional light could be the sun.

If you're not really going vertically up, you're not going into space, you can't really get any nearer to the sun; then you could think of that as a directional light and most of the time, that is thought of as a directional light in a lot of games.

Again, it depends on what sort of game you're playing. If you're playing a game where you can go into space and you can get to the stars or the sun, then that really wouldn't be a directional light; that would be a different light. But more different types of light will be covered in different sections. So let's implement this by using the shaders/lighting.frag file, as shown in the following code:

```
struct Light
{
  //vec3 position;
  vec3 direction;

  vec3 ambient;
  vec3 diffuse;
  vec3 specular;
};
```

What we are doing is commenting out an original position, vec3 position, and instead adding a direction, that is, vec3 direction.

In the diffuse lighting, we need to modify it slightly:

```
// Diffuse
vec3 norm = normalize(Normal);
// vec3 lightDir = normalize(light.position - FragPos);
vec3 lightDir = normalize(-light.direction);
float diff = max(dot(norm, lightDir), 0.0);
vec3 diffuse = light.diffuse * diff * vec3(texture(material.diffuse, TexCoords));
```

So, let's just comment out lightDir because though we're going to have a light direction again, we want to leave in this code in case we need it later on. So, add a new code line, lightDir = normalize -light.direction.

So that's all we have to do here, because we're not working out the difference between the position (light.position) and the actual fragment shader position (FragPos). We don't have to do that, because all we are concerned about is the light's direction.

Types of light sources and combining of lights

Making changes to main code to integrate directional light in our world

Now open the `main.cpp` file, which is used for the actual light and the shaders. Comment out our shader programs, because we're not going to actually use the lamp shader in this section, simply because we don't want any sort of light source with an origin position:

```
// Build and compile our shader program
  Shader lightingShader( "res/shaders/lighting.vs",
  "res/shaders/lighting.frag" );
  //Shader lampShader( "res/shaders/lamp.vs", "res/shaders/lamp.frag" );
```

Here we're going to use an array of different cube positions.

```
// Positions all containers
  glm::vec3 cubePositions[] = {
  glm::vec3( 0.0f, 0.0f, 0.0f),
  glm::vec3( 2.0f, 5.0f, -15.0f),
  glm::vec3( -1.5f, -2.2f, -2.5f),
  glm::vec3( -3.8f, -2.0f, -12.3f),
  glm::vec3( 2.4f, -0.4f, -3.5f),
  glm::vec3( -1.7f, 3.0f, -7.5f),
  glm::vec3( 1.3f, -2.0f, -2.5f),
  glm::vec3( 1.5f, 2.0f, -2.5f),
  glm::vec3( 1.5f, 0.2f, -1.5f),
  glm::vec3( -1.3f, 1.0f, -1.5f)
  };
```

We're going to spawn several cubes, very similar to what we've done before, and you can see the variance in having different cubes. We don't need the light vertex array object anymore because we're not doing the lamp shader, so let's just comment that out:

```
/*
  // Then, we set the light's VAO (VBO stays the same. After all, the
  vertices are the same for the light object (also a 3D cube))
  GLuint lightVAO;
  glGenVertexArrays(1, &lightVAO);
  glBindVertexArray(lightVAO);
  // We only need to bind to the VBO (to link it with
  glVertexAttribPointer), no need to fill it; the VBO's data already contains
  all we need.
  glBindBuffer(GL_ARRAY_BUFFER, VBO);
  // Set the vertex attributes (only position data for the lamp))
  glVertexAttribPointer(0, 3, GL_FLOAT, GL_FALSE, 8 * sizeof(GLfloat),
  (GLvoid*)0); // Note that we skip over the other data in our buffer object
  (we don't need the normals/textures, only positions).
```

```
    glEnableVertexAttribArray(0);
    glBindVertexArray(0);
    */
```

All this looks good so far, but we've to do a few changes within the `while` loop, to the part where we're using the lighting shader. So, add `GLint lightDirLoc = glGetUniformLocation` and `glUniform3f`:

```
    // Use cooresponding shader when setting uniforms/drawing objects
    lightingShader.Use( );
    //GLint lightPosLoc = glGetUniformLocation(lightingShader.Program,
    "light.position");
    GLint lightDirLoc = glGetUniformLocation( lightingShader.Program,
    "light.direction" );
    GLint viewPosLoc = glGetUniformLocation( lightingShader.Program, "viewPos"
    );
    //glUniform3f(lightPosLoc, lightPos.x, lightPos.y, lightPos.z);
    glUniform3f( lightDirLoc, -0.2f, -1.0f, -0.3f );
    glUniform3f( viewPosLoc, camera.GetPosition( ).x   , camera.GetPosition(
    ).y, camera.GetPosition( ).z );
```

The view position location, which is just the camera's position, is fine. The ambient and the diffuse need not be changed. You can modify them if you want to, but it's not needed for this particular chapter.

Now, create a for loop as follows:

```
    // Draw 10 containers with the same VAO and VBO information;
    // only their world space coordinates differ
    glm::mat4 model;
    glBindVertexArray( boxVAO );
    for ( GLuint i = 0; i < 10; i++)
    {
    model = glm::mat4( );
    model = glm::translate( model, cubePositions[i] );
    GLfloat angle = 20.0f * i;
    model = glm::rotate( model, angle, glm::vec3( 1.0f, 0.3f, 0.5f ) );
    glUniformMatrix4fv( modelLoc, 1, GL_FALSE, glm::value_ptr( model ) );

    glDrawArrays( GL_TRIANGLES, 0, 36 );
    }
    glBindVertexArray( 0 );
```

Types of light sources and combining of lights

Here, we add `glm::mat4` as a 4x4 matrix. We will call it model. Then we add `glBindVertexArray`, which will take the box vertex array object. Sometimes we only want one cube; sometimes we want several, so we will use `cubePositions` and it will take the iterator as the index. Now we're going to add `GLfloat angle = 20.0f * i; model = glm::rotate` and for the rotation, it's going to take the model again. For the angle, we are just going to put angle. After that, we will add a vector,`glm::vec3`, and for this, we are just going to put `1.0f, 0.3f`, and `0.5f`. We're just going to uniform the 4x4 matrix. Use `glUniformMatrix4fv`, because its four float values and `modelLoc`, which is what we created previously, will take the value 1. Then add `GL_FALSE` and `glm::value_ptr (model)`. `glDrawArrays` will take `GL_TRIANGLES`, the starting index 0, and 36 different vertices. So, if we put a semicolon there, we just need to `glBind` the vertex array to 0, so we will just unbind it.

Now we will run this bad boy and we get **Build Failed**. This is happening because we commented out the light vertex array object and hence there's no need for us to use `glDeleteVertexArrays( 1, &lightVAO )`. So, now run it again and you will get **Build Succeeded** and the following output:

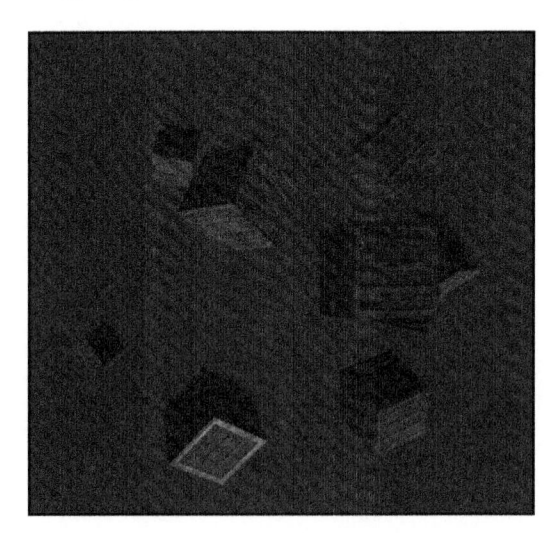

Here, we've got our different objects. All of these objects are affected by the light in the same way. Obviously, there are angle differences, and that's what makes the intensity of the light affecting it different. But in terms of their position, that doesn't matter. Because the light is coming from one direction, the objects are affected exactly the same. They are just as dark and bright. The specular lighting will affect them just the same way, and it's the angle that makes the lighting affect it differently.

So far, we have learned about directional lights in modern OpenGL. We'll cover an advanced form of lighting in the next section where we'll create some really, really cool stuff with lighting. When you see all our games, especially games that look really, really good in terms of graphical fidelity, you'll find that when you start going under the layers and start doing programming in graphics, you'll see a lot of it's due to lighting.

The way lighting affects things has probably the biggest effect because by using normal lighting you can make an object look like it's got depth, even though it's just a flat texture, and that is pretty radical.

Point lights

In this chapter, we will discuss point lights. We've covered lighting systems in a bit of depth so far. One technique is directional lights, which essentially are light sources that point in a certain direction, hence the name directional light; but they do not have an original location, that is, they are infinitely far away. So, say for example, we have two objects that are exactly the same, rotated exactly the same way, and there's no other lighting affecting those objects; no matter how far they are away from each other, they will not be affected differently by the directional light source.

The point light concept

A **point light** is a light that has an actual origin, and it emits the light in every single direction:

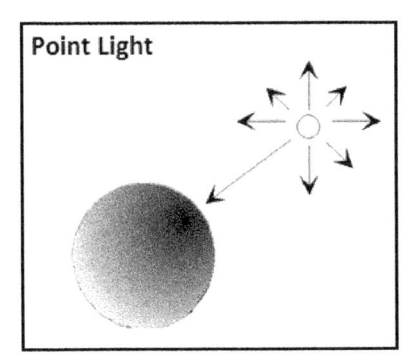

Types of light sources and combining of lights

You can almost think of a point light like our sun or a star in real life. You could argue that the sun technically emits different amounts of light from different sides, but we could, for argument's sake, say it emits the same intensity, the same type of light from its origin in all directions. It's very common for, let's say, space games to have something like a point light as the sun, a star, or some other sort of object like that.

First of all, just open your lighting fragment shader, that is, ../shaders/lighting.frag, and in this file, we need to modify a few things:

```
struct Light
{
  //vec3 direction;
  vec3 position;

  vec3 ambient;
  vec3 diffuse;
  vec3 specular;

  float constant;
  float linear;
  float quadratic;
};
```

In the preceding code snippet, we will comment out the direction vector because we don't need the direction anymore since the lighting source has a position, and it just emits light in every direction. So, ambient, diffuse, and specular will need no changes. Now, we will add a constant, a linear, and a quadratic float. That's all for the lighting struct.

The diffuse section

Now, let's check out the diffuse section:

```
// Diffuse
  vec3 norm = normalize(Normal);
  vec3 lightDir = normalize(light.position - FragPos);
  //vec3 lightDir = normalize(-light.direction);
  float diff = max(dot(norm, lightDir), 0.0);
  vec3 diffuse = light.diffuse * diff * vec3(texture(material.diffuse, TexCoords));
```

We're still going to normalize our Normal, but we want the difference between the light position and the fragment position. So we'll comment out the light direction, vec3 lightDir = normalize(-light.direction) and we'll uncomment light.position - FragPos.

The difference, `max (dot( norm, lightDir)`, will be kept as it is. In terms of `diffuse`, we're still using `light.diffuse`, multiplying it by the `float diffuse` variable, `diff`, and then `vec3`.

The specular section

Let's look at the specular section now:

```
// Specular
vec3 viewDir = normalize(viewPos - FragPos);
vec3 reflectDir = reflect(-lightDir, norm);
float spec = pow(max(dot(viewDir, reflectDir), 0.0),
material.shininess);
vec3 specular = light.specular * spec *
vec3(texture(material.specular, TexCoords));
```

Here, the view direction and the reflection direction won't change. What we need to add is something called attenuation, something like, distance and lighting.

The attenuation section

Attenuation is essentially dropout. Attenuation lighting is a decrease in lighting as you move away from an object. Take a look at this image:

We've got four different light sources, **A**, **B**, **C**, and **D**. We will assume they're all the same. **A** has more of an effect on the ground than **D** because **D** is further away. So, basically attenuation is the fall-off.

Types of light sources and combining of lights

So, let's implement it:

```
// Attenuation
float distance = length(light.position - FragPos);
float attenuation = 1.0f / (light.constant + light.linear * distance
+ light.quadratic * (distance * distance));
```

In the preceding code snippet, if the light source was further away but still had the same sort of angle, it would still affect our object the same, and we don't want that. So, we will add `float distance = length(light.position - FragPos)`, and after that, add `float attenuation = 1.0f / (light.constant + light.linear * distance + light.quadratic * (distance * distance))`. So, this is how we calculated the distance and the attenuation.

> If you want more information about how this works, feel free to check out the following links:
> - https://open.gl
> - https://learnopengl.com
>
> These are great resources, so feel free to check them out.

Now we are going to add attenuation to the ambient, diffuse, and specular lights:

```
// Attenuation
float distance = length(light.position - FragPos);
float attenuation = 1.0f / (light.constant + light.linear *
distance + light.quadratic * (distance * distance));

ambient *= attenuation;
diffuse *= attenuation;
specular *= attenuation;
```

We need these because all three of them will have attenuation factored in as they need to factor in distance.

Time for changes in main.cpp

Open the `main.cpp` file. We will have to do a few modifications to it. The first thing we need to actually uncomment out is `lampShader`:

```
// Build and compile our shader program
Shader lightingShader( "res/shaders/lighting.vs",
"res/shaders/lighting.frag" );
```

```
Shader lampShader( "res/shaders/lamp.vs", "res/shaders/lamp.frag" );
```

This is because we're using the lamp again since we are dealing with the point light.

The next thing we need to change is the light vertex array object because we're using the lamp shader now. So, uncomment the following code block:

```
GLuint VBO, boxVAO;
glGenVertexArrays( 1, &boxVAO );
glGenBuffers( 1, &VBO );

glBindBuffer( GL_ARRAY_BUFFER, VBO );
glBufferData( GL_ARRAY_BUFFER, sizeof(vertices),
vertices, GL_STATIC_DRAW );

glBindVertexArray( boxVAO );
glVertexAttribPointer( 0, 3, GL_FLOAT, GL_FALSE, 8 *
sizeof( GLfloat ), ( GLvoid * )0 );
glEnableVertexAttribArray(0);
glVertexAttribPointer( 1, 3, GL_FLOAT, GL_FALSE, 8 *
sizeof( GLfloat ), ( GLvoid * )( 3 * sizeof( GLfloat ) ) );
glEnableVertexAttribArray( 1 );
glVertexAttribPointer( 2, 2, GL_FLOAT, GL_FALSE, 8 *
sizeof( GLfloat ), ( GLvoid * )( 6 * sizeof( GLfloat ) ) );
glEnableVertexAttribArray( 2 );
glBindVertexArray( 0 );
```

Now we need an emission map, so we will add `emissionMap`:

```
// Load textures
GLuint diffuseMap, specularMap, emissionMap;
glGenTextures( 1, &diffuseMap );
glGenTextures( 1, &specularMap );
glGenTextures( 1, &emissionMap );
```

The only change we need to make now is actually within our `while` loop:

```
lightingShader.Use( );

GLint lightPosLoc = glGetUniformLocation( lightingShader.Program,
"light.position" );
//GLint lightDirLoc = glGetUniformLocation( lightingShader.Program,
//"light.direction" );
GLint viewPosLoc = glGetUniformLocation( lightingShader.Program,
"viewPos" );
glUniform3f( lightPosLoc, lightPos.x, lightPos.y, lightPos.z );
//glUniform3f( lightPosLoc, -02.f, 1.0f, -0.3f );
glUniform3f( viewPosLoc, camera.GetPosition( ).x, camera.GetPosition( ).y,
```

Types of light sources and combining of lights

```
    camera.GetPosition( ).z );
```

So, as shown in the preceding code snippet, in the lighting shader, uncomment the line: `GLint lightPosLoc = glGetUniformLocation( lightingShader.Program, "light.position" );` and comment out the directions, `GLint lightDirLoc = glGetUniformLocation( lightingShader.Program, "light.direction" );`, because again, the pointer light emits light in every direction. Also, don't forget to comment out `glUniform3f( lightPosLoc, -02.f, 1.0f, -0.3f );` and remove the comment from `glUniform3f( lightPosLoc, lightPos.x, lightPos.y, lightPos.z );`.

Now, we also need to add the constants, the linear, and the quadratic, which are float values:

```
// Set lights properties
 glUniform3f( glGetUniformLocation( lightingShader.Program, "light.ambient"
), 0.2f, 0.2f, 0.2f );
 glUniform3f( glGetUniformLocation( lightingShader.Program, "light.diffuse"
), 0.5f, 0.5f, 0.5f );
 glUniform3f( glGetUniformLocation( lightingShader.Program,
"light.specular" ), 1.0f, 1.0f, 1.0f );
 glUniform1f( glGetUniformLocation( lightingShader.Program,
"light.constant" ), 1.0f );
 glUniform1f( glGetUniformLocation( lightingShader.Program, "light.linear"
), 0.09 );
 glUniform1f( glGetUniformLocation( lightingShader.Program,
"light.quadratic" ), 0.032 );
```

Now, in order to bind our textures, we need to uncomment out the `lampShader.Use( )` block. Also, delete the light vertex array object, that is, uncomment the `glDeleteVertexArrays( 1, &lightVAO );` line:

```
    glDeleteVertexArrays( 1, &boxVAO );
    glDeleteVertexArrays( 1, &lightVAO );
    glDeleteBuffers( 1, &VBO );
```

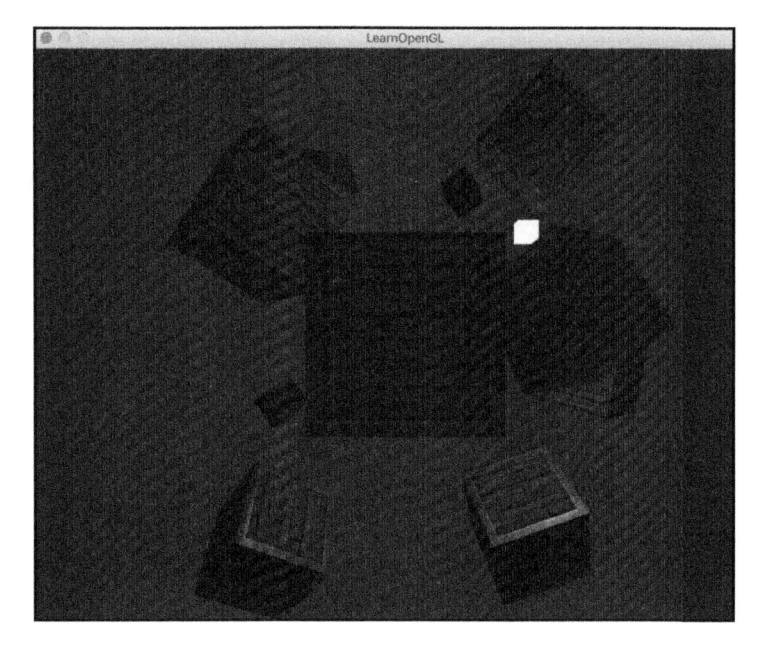

Now, we are ready to run our application and we get the following screen:

If you examine the output, we've got our original light source and the objects that are further away are a bit darker, as they should be.

But let's make one more change in main.cpp; we can actually move our light by uncommenting the following lines in the while loop:

- lightPos.x -=0.005f;
- lightPos.z -=0.005f;

[159]

Types of light sources and combining of lights

And now, if you re-run the application, as you can see in the following screenshot, attenuation is factored in. You can see that this object is getting slightly brighter now, and you'll actually start seeing this particular object getting brighter:

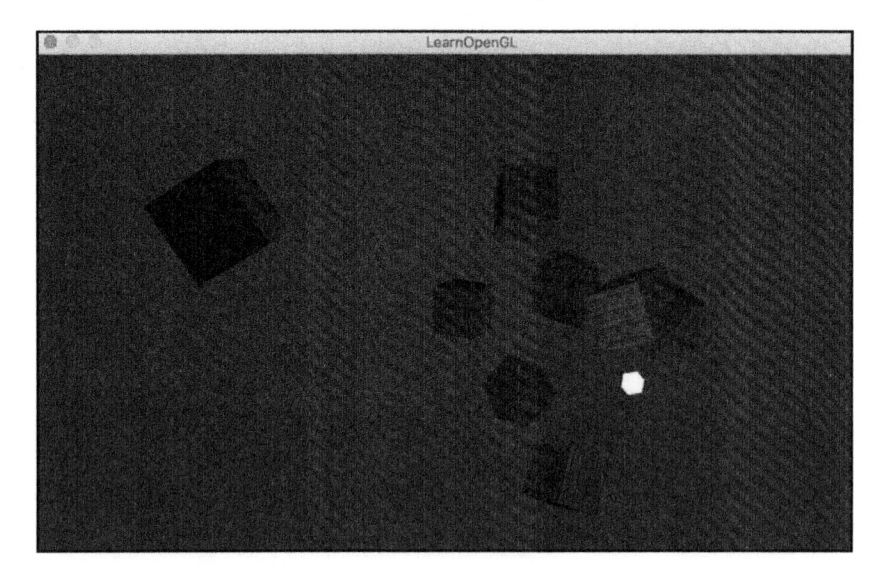

Now, again comment out the following lines back in the `while` loop:

- `lightPos.x -=0.005f;`
- `lightPos.z -=0.005f;`

And, instead we will try changing the light position in the camera section:

```
// Camera
Camera camera( glm::vec3( 0.0f, 0.0f, 3.0f ) );
GLfloat lastX = WIDTH / 2.0;
GLfloat lastY = HEIGHT / 2.0;
bool keys[1024];
bool firstMouse = true;

// Light attributes
glm::vec3 lightPos( 1.2f, 1.0f, -2.0f );
```

[160]

So, as you can see in the preceding code, we have replaced `2.0f` to `-2.0f` in the light attributes section. Now, if you run your application, you can see the light is being emitted in every single direction. Nearer objects are brighter than more distant objects:

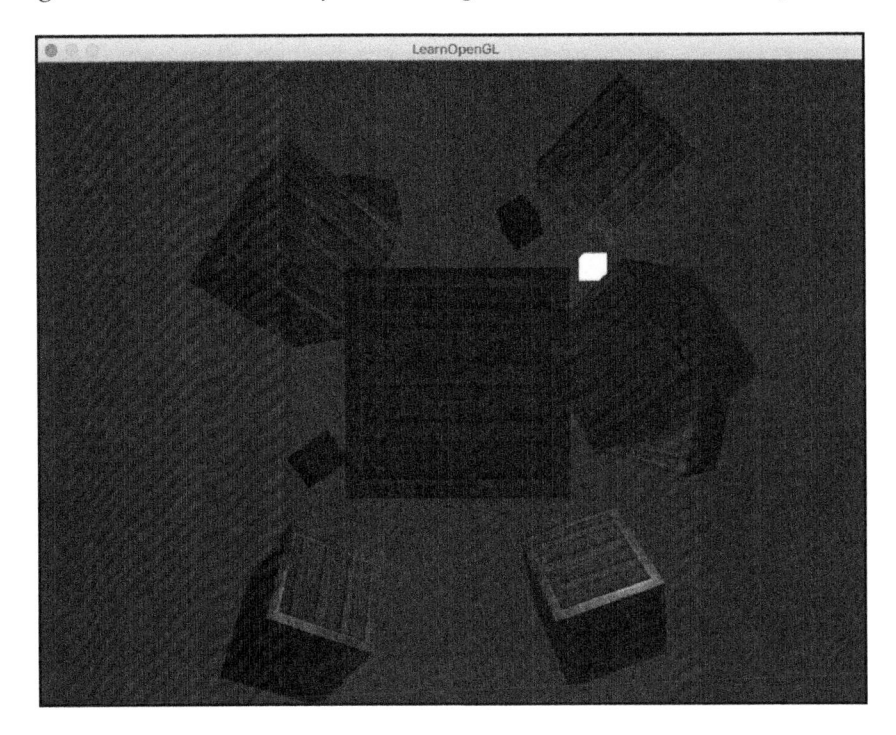

So, that is it for point lights.

Spotlight

Let's discuss and take a look at how we can add spotlights to our game. We've looked at directional lights, we've looked at point lights. Directional lights have a direction but they don't have an original position, so they are infinitely far away. A point light has a position but it shines light in every single direction, whereas a spotlight has a position and a direction.

Types of light sources and combining of lights

Take a look at the following diagram of a spotlight:

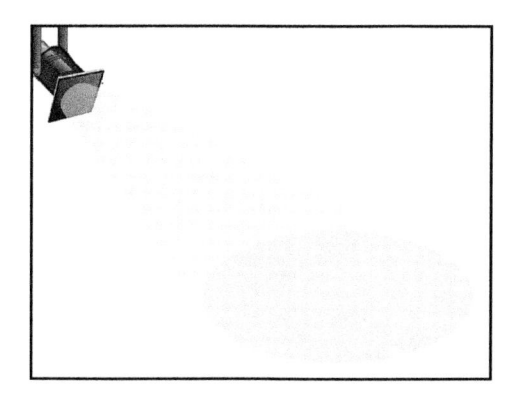

So, the position of the light is high up somewhere, and you can also see that there is a direction for the light. It essentially creates a cone-like effect, sort of what a lamp or a torch would do. Spotlights are used on stages. But spotlights are used in several scenarios in games throughout your world.

So, without further ado, let's get on with coding our spotlights.

Making changes to shader files

Follow the below mentioned steps:

1. Updating shader files is actually very, very simple. We only need to actually modify the lighting fragment shader in terms of the shader files; everything else looks fine. In `lighting.frag`, we can keep the `Material` struct as it is because it's got `diffuse`, `specular`, and `shininess`, and that's what we require for a spot light.
2. But with the light struct, we need the direction because the spotlight has an original position and a direction in which it is shining. So, we'll uncomment `vec3 direction`. We also need a couple of float variables. The first one is `float cutOff`. The next one is `float outerCutOff`. Take a look at the following code:

```
#version 330 core
struct Material
{
    sampler2D diffuse;
    sampler2D specular;
    float shininess;
```

[162]

```
};
struct Light
{
    vec3 position;
    vec3 direction;
    float cutOff;
    float outerCutOff;

    float constant;
    float linear;
    float quadratic;

    vec3 ambient;
    vec3 diffuse;
    vec3 specular;
};
```

3. The rest of the terms till `void main` starts remain the same.
4. In `void main`, the ambient calculation, the diffuse calculation, and the specular calculation aren't changing. Even the attenuation calculation isn't going to be changing. All we actually need to do is add an extra section for the spotlight, which is going to be calculating soft edges.
5. So, for the calculation of the soft edges, we're going to add `float theta = dot();`, and to this we are going to pass `lightDir`. This needs to be normalized, so we're passing `normalize()`. And then finally, here you need to specify `-light.direction`. You need to add a negative light value because you're doing it from the perspective of the camera, not from the user. That's the reason the position is negated. On the other line, we need to calculate the difference between `cutOff` and `outerCutOff`, so we'll add the following:

    ```
    float epsilon = (light.cutOff - light.outerCutOff);
    ```

6. Then add `float intensity = clamp();`. And in here, we are going to pass `theta - light.outerCutOff`. We want to divide this calculation by `epsilon` and then just put two values, `0.0` and `1.0`:

    ```
    float intensity = clamp((theta - light.outerCutOff) / epsilon, 0.0, 1.0);
    ```

7. Finally, we just need to add the intensity into `diffuse` and `specular`:

    ```
    diffuse *= intensity;
    specular *= intensity;
    ```

So, we're now actually done with the updating the shader.

Types of light sources and combining of lights

Minor modification to Camera.h

In this section, we'll need `GetFront`, which is a private variable in our main code. We'll make a minor modification for it in our `Camera.h` file. So, below the `glm::vec3 GetPosition()` method, we'll add a simple method as follows:

```
glm::vec3 GetFront()
{
    return this -> front;
}
```

Making changes to the main code

Now, if we go to main.cpp, we'll make the following modifications:

1. We don't need `lampShader` because we're going to be doing it via a spotlight, so we'll comment out the code. The reason we don't need any sort of lamp shader or anything like that is because what we're going to do in this section is attach the spotlight to, essentially, the camera. You can almost think of it like those helmets with the light on top that people use for rock climbing and that sort of stuff. We're simply going to simulate that because directional light and point lights are great and if you have them static, they're easy to see and understand what is going on. With a spotlight, it really does help if you can move it, and the best way to move it is with the camera.
2. We'll comment out the light vertex array object as we don't need it anymore.
3. After we've commented that out, we can go directly into the while loop and we need to change a few things here. When we go to `lightingShader.Use`, we need to change some of the code there. We're going to add `GLint lightSpotDirLocation = glGetUniformLocation();`. In here, we need to pass `lightingShader.Program`, and the other parameter you need to specify is `"light.direction"`. What we are going to do next is duplicate the preceding code and make the following modifications to it:

```
lightingShader.Use();
GLint lightPosLoc = glGetUniformLocation( lightingShader.Program,
"light.position" );
GLint lightSpotdirLoc = glGetUniformLocation(
lightingShader.Program, "light.direction" );
GLint lightSpotCutOffLoc = glGetUniformLocation(
lightingShader.Program, "light.cutOff" );
GLint lightSpotOuterCutOffLoc = glGetUniformLocation(
lightingShader.Program, "light.outerCutOff" );
```

```
        GLint viewPosLoc = glGetUniformLocation( lightingShader.Program,
    "viewPos" );
        glUniform3f( lightPosLoc, camera.GetPosition( ).x,
    camera.GetPosition( ).y, camera.GetPosition( ).z);
        glUniform3f( lightSpotdirLoc, camera.GetFront( ).x,
    camera.GetFront( ).y, camera.GetFront( ).z);
        glUniform1f( lightSpotCutOffLoc, glm::cos( glm::radians( 12.5f ) )
    );
        glUniform1f( lightSpotOuterCutOffLoc, glm::cos( glm::radians(
    17.5f ) ) );
        glUniform3f( viewPosLoc, camera.GetPosition( ).x,
    camera.GetPosition( ).y, camera.GetPosition( ).z);
```

4. We'll modify the remaining terms of `lightingShader` code where we set the light properties as follows:

    ```
    glUniform3f( glGetUniformLocation( lightingShader.Program,
    "light.ambient" ),    0.1f, 0.1f, 0.1f );
    glUniform3f( glGetUniformLocation( lightingShader.Program,
    "light.diffuse" ), 0.8f, 0.8f, 0.8f );
    ```

5. There's only one thing we're going to change in here now. We'll comment out the whole `lampShader` code. Because we commented out the declaration and initialization, we need to do the same here.

6. We also need to comment out `glDeleteVertexArrays();`.

We're all ready to run this now. You will see similar output on your screen. So, as you can see, we've got some light. The spot light is attached to us.

Types of light sources and combining of lights

So, if we move forward, as you can see, we've got sort of a spotlight effect, and it's more profound the closer we get to it, as seen in the following screenshot:

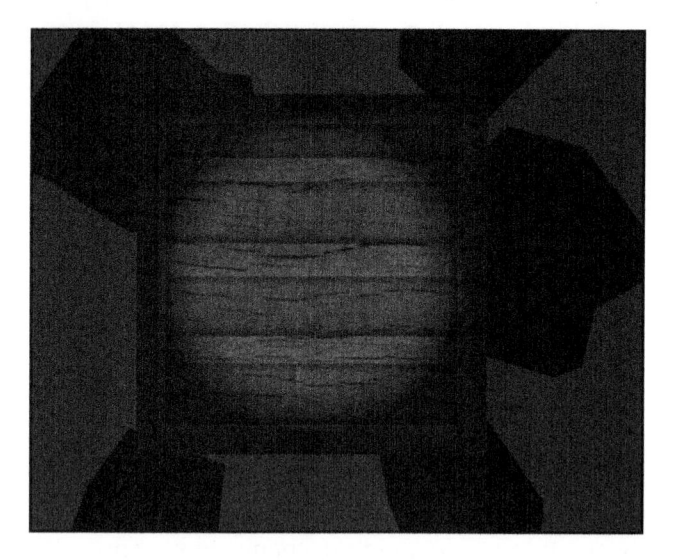

Otherwise, it's very wide as we move further away from the objects, as seen in the following screenshot:

Hence, they're smaller. As we look around, we get a sort of spotlight effect. As you can see, it affects objects that are further away slightly differently, and we have this really cool spotlight, as seen in the following screenshot:

Let's try and do it on a corner, as follows:

We've got this really cool spotlight that is attached to our head. You could go ahead and create some sort of building game or some sort of miner's game where you have a light on your head. That would be pretty cool.

Combining light

In this section, we're going to be looking at combining our light sources. So far we've covered directional lights, point lights, and spotlights in the previous sections. The following is a brief overview of what they are:

- **Directional light**: A directional light is a light that has a particular direction. It shines light in a particular direction. But it doesn't have a location, a position. It's just infinitely far away from everything.
- **Point light**: A point light has a position, but it shines light in every single direction. Depending on what you're doing and what sort of game you've got, you could potentially have the sun or a star' as a directional light, but if you could go into space, go around your star or get near it, then you'd probably want a point light.
- **Spotlight**: A spotlight essentially is like a lamp. It casts a light in an initial position, and then in a direction as well. So it's like a combination of the preceding two types of light.

In the previous sections, we looked at all of them, but at the moment, in these sections, we've just been covering them one at a time. We've either been commenting out code or modifying code to just show one realistically. But in a real game scenario or a free application scenario, you'll want multiple light sources. You'll want multiple instances of directional lights, point lights, and spotlights. You'll probably want to try and create your own really cool effects as well. In this section, we're going to be combining our three types of light casters.

As usual, we'll start by updating the shader files.

Getting the shader files ready

Take a look at the below mentioned steps:

1. The first thing that we need to do is go to the fragment shader for lighting, `lighting.frag`. That's the only shader that we actually need to modify, so we won't touch `lighting.vs`. Check out the following steps to understand the changes that we need to make to the fragment shader:
2. So, first of all, we're going to add `#define`, and this is just going to be `NUMBER_OF_POINT_LIGHTS`. For our project, we'll add the value as 4 because we're going to have four point lights.

Chapter 5

3. Next, we're going to need a data type for three different types of light source: a directional light, a point light, and a spotlight. For that, what we'll do is actually duplicate the struct that we already have in code. We'll rename each one of them appropriately: `DirLight` for directional light, `PointLight` for point light, and `SpotLight` for the spot light. We don't need all of the vectors and the floats that we've got in the structs. Take a look at the following code to understand all the changes we need to make in the new struct that we have defined:

```
version 330 core
#define NUMBER_OF_POINT_LIGHTS 4
struct Material
{
    sampler2D diffuse;
    sampler2D specular;
    float shininess;
};
```

4. The directional light, as you may remember, doesn't have a position, it has a direction. It has an ambient, diffuse, and specular, but it doesn't have any of the float variables: constant linear and quadratic. So we'll just remove them:

```
struct DirLight
{
    vec3 direction;

    vec3 ambient;
    vec3 diffuse;
    vec3 specular;
};
```

5. For the point light, remember it doesn't have a direction; it has a position because it just emits light in every direction. We can get rid of `cutOff` and `outerCutOff`, but we're going to need everything else:

```
struct PointLight
{
    vec3 position;

    float constant;
    float linear;
    float quadratic;

    vec3 ambient;
    vec3 diffuse;
    vec3 specular;
};
```

Types of light sources and combining of lights

6. For the spotlight, nothing will be changing in here because this structure was created in the previous section, which covered spotlights:

    ```
    struct SpotLight
    {
        vec3 position;
        vec3 direction;
        float cutOff;
        float outerCutOff;

        float constant;
        float linear;
        float quadratic;

        vec3 ambient;
        vec3 diffuse;
        vec3 specular;
    };
    ```

7. As we move down, uniform Light light is going to change slightly as we've got three different sources of light. So we'll make the following changes to it:

    ```
    uniform DirLight dirLight;
    uniform PointLight pointLights[NUMBER_OF_POINT_LIGHTS];
    uniform SpotLight spotLight;
    uniform Material material;
    ```

    In the preceding code, for a PointLight as you may remember, we created a #define. So, the uniform PointLight is going to be an array of lights. Even though we're creating multiple spotlights and only one directional light and spotlight, you can create multiple directional lights and you can create multiple spotlights such as lamps, lights on a stick and that sort of thing. You might have one really strong source of light such as a directional light that could be simulating the sun, and then you might have just other general small lights.

8. What we need to do next is create some function prototypes because at the moment, what we've been doing is just doing everything in main. This has been alright for now, but we need a bit more flexibility with the way we're doing things. So, we're going to add vec3 CalcDirLight();, and this is going to take a few parameters such as DirLight. Then we're going to take a vec3 for the normal. We've explained the use of all of these different vectors and properties before. Again, we're just combining what we've done over the past few sections. And then, we'll duplicate the code and make the following highlighted changes to it:

```
// Function prototypes
vec3 CalcDirLight( DirLight light, vec3 normal, vec3 viewDir );
vec3 CalcPointLight( PointLight light, vec3 normal, vec3 fragPos,
vec3 viewDir );
vec3 CalcSpotLight( SpotLight light, vec3 normal, vec3 fragPos,
vec3 viewDir );
```

Making modifications void main of lighting.frag

Check out the following steps to understand the modifications:

1. In the void main of `lighting.frag`, we're going to get rid of all the initially present code and add fresh code to it. We'll start by adding `vec3` normal. We're just going to be normalizing using `Normal`.

2. Then we're going to create a vec3 for `viewDir`. This is going to normalize the difference between `viewPos` and `FragPos`.

3. Now we need to do the directional lighting calculation. With this, we're just going to be calling the `CalcDirLight` method. So, we're not going to be doing much code in main. Because we're adding more stuff to it, it's becoming like another C++ project because we are abstracting it out into different methods, so we can reuse this code when and where we need to. So, we'll add `vec3 result` and we'll assign the value of `CalcDirLight();`, and this is going to take the `dirLight` variable, the `norm` that we've just calculated, and the `viewDir`.

4. Next, we're just going to loop over the point lights, then factor them in. So, add a for loop and pass the initializing parameters, `int i = 0; i < NUMBER_OF_POINT_LIGHTS; i++`. In the `for` loop we are going to add `result += CalcPointLight()`. Again, what we're doing now is adding the effect of the different point lights to our result because again, this lighting is affecting our particular object, and this is the way it's done. So, to `CalcPointLight()` we're going to pass `pointLights[i]`, `norm`, and `FragPos`.

5. What we're going to do now is add the code for the spotlight. So, we'll factor in the spotlight and add `result += CalcSpotLight()`. And this simply takes in the `spotLight` variable, `norm`, `FragPos`, and `viewDir`. Then we'll add `color = vec4(result, 1.0);`. Take a look at the following code to understand the description:

```
void main( )
{
    // Properties
```

Types of light sources and combining of lights

```
vec3 norm = normalize( Normal );
vec3 viewDir = normalize( viewPos - FragPos );

// Directional lighting
vec3 result = CalcDirLight( dirLight, norm, viewDir );

// Point lights
for ( int i = 0; i < NUMBER_OF_POINT_LIGHTS; i++ )
{
result += CalcPointLight( pointLights[i], norm, FragPos, viewDir
);
}

// Spot light
result += CalcSpotLight( spotLight, norm, FragPos, viewDir );

color = vec4( result, 1.0 );
}
```

6. This is all stuff we've done before, and we're just abstracting it out now.
7. Now let's do the calculation of colors for the different sources of light. So here, what we'll do is copy and paste the `vec3 calc` code for all three sources of light. Now let's do the directional light calculation. So to the `vec3 CalcDirLight()` method we'll add `vec3 lightDir`, and this is going to equal to `normalize( - light.direction );`.

The reason for `-light.direction` is because we're not doing it from our object, we're doing it from the light. So, instead of the way the object is looking at the light, it's coming from the light. So, that's the reason why it's flipped.

8. And now we need to add float. This is going to be the diffuse shading. So, `diff = max ()`, and to `max ()` we'll pass `dot ( normal, lightDir )`, `0.0`.
9. Next, we're going to be calculating the specular shading. So add `vec3 reflectDir = reflect ()`, and to `reflect ()` we'll pass `-lightDir, normal`.
10. Then we'll add `float spec = pow ()`, and to that we'll pass `max ()`, and to `max ()` we'll pass `dot ( viewDir, reflectDir )` and `0.0`.
11. Finally, we need to add `material.shininess`. Now we need to combine the results. So, add `vec3 ambient = light.ambient * vec3 ();`, and to `vec3 ()` we'll pass `texture ( material.diffuse, TexCoords )`. This is going to be the texture diffuse and the texture coordinates, and for the diffuse and specular light it's similar to ambient light, so make the highlighted changes to in the following code. Also, take a look at the following code to understand the preceding description:

```
vec3 CalcDirLight( DirLight light, vec3 normal, vec3 viewDir )
{
 vec3 lightDir = normalize( -light.direction );

 // Diffuse shading
 float diff = max( dot( normal, lightDir ), 0.0 );

 // Specular shading
 vec3 reflectDir = reflect( -lightDir, normal );
 float spec = pow( max( dot( viewDir, reflectDir ), 0.0 ),
material.shininess );

 // Combine results
 vec3 ambient = light.ambient * vec3( texture( material.diffuse,
TexCoords ) );
 vec3 diffuse = light.diffuse * diff * vec3( texture(
material.diffuse, TexCoords ) );
 vec3 specular = light.specular * spec * vec3( texture(
material.specular, TexCoords ) );

 return ( ambient + diffuse + specular );
}
```

In the preceding code, we just need to return the calculation, which is `ambient + diffuse + specular`.

12. Now we need to calculate the point light, so what we'll do is duplicate the lines of code mentioned in the previous steps and paste in the `CalcPointLight()` method; we'll add, change, and remove what we need to. Take a look at the following highlighted code to understand the changes:

```
// Calculates the color when using a point light.
vec3 CalcPointLight( PointLight light, vec3 normal, vec3 fragPos,
vec3 viewDir )
{
 vec3 lightDir = normalize( light.position - fragPos );

 // Diffuse shading
 float diff = max( dot( normal, lightDir ), 0.0 );

 // Specular shading
 vec3 reflectDir = reflect( -lightDir, normal );
 float spec = pow( max( dot( viewDir, reflectDir ), 0.0 ),
material.shininess );

 // Attenuation
 float distance = length( light.position - fragPos );
```

Types of light sources and combining of lights

```
    float attenuation = 1.0f / ( light.constant + light.linear *
distance + light.quadratic * ( distance * distance ) );

    // Combine results
    vec3 ambient = light.ambient * vec3( texture( material.diffuse,
TexCoords ) );
    vec3 diffuse = light.diffuse * diff * vec3( texture(
material.diffuse, TexCoords ) );
    vec3 specular = light.specular * spec * vec3( texture(
material.specular, TexCoords ) );

    ambient *= attenuation;
    diffuse *= attenuation;
    specular *= attenuation;

    return ( ambient + diffuse + specular );
}
```

In the preceding code, after defining the `specular` shading we added the attenuation code, as we need to factor in the attenuation.

13. Now we need to do the calculations for the `spotlight ()` method. Again, we're just going to copy and paste the previous code because we'll most likely be adding quite a lot to it, but we'll need most of it. So take a look at the following highlighted code:

```
// Calculates the color when using a spot light.
vec3 CalcSpotLight( SpotLight light, vec3 normal, vec3 fragPos,
vec3 viewDir )
{
    vec3 lightDir = normalize( light.position - fragPos );

    // Diffuse shading
    float diff = max( dot( normal, lightDir ), 0.0 );

    // Specular shading
    vec3 reflectDir = reflect( -lightDir, normal );
    float spec = pow( max( dot( viewDir, reflectDir ), 0.0 ),
material.shininess );

    // Attenuation
    float distance = length( light.position - fragPos );
    float attenuation = 1.0f / ( light.constant + light.linear *
distance + light.quadratic * ( distance * distance ) );

    // Spotlight intensity
    float theta = dot( lightDir, normalize( -light.direction ) );
```

[174]

Chapter 5

```
        float epsilon = light.cutOff - light.outerCutOff;
        float intensity = clamp( ( theta - light.outerCutOff ) / epsilon,
0.0, 1.0 );

        // Combine results
        vec3 ambient = light.ambient * vec3( texture( material.diffuse,
TexCoords ) );
        vec3 diffuse = light.diffuse * diff * vec3( texture(
material.diffuse, TexCoords ) );
        vec3 specular = light.specular * spec * vec3( texture(
material.specular, TexCoords ) );

        ambient *= attenuation * intensity;
        diffuse *= attenuation * intensity;
        specular *= attenuation * intensity;

        return ( ambient + diffuse + specular );
    }
```

In the preceding code, before we go on to the `ambient`, `diffuse`, and `specular` vectors, we needed to add the spotlight intensity calculation code. Take a good look at the highlighted code. Then, finally, we just need to factor in the intensity. So we just multiplied the attenuation by the intensity in the final lines of code.

We're done now updating the fragment lighting shader. We've covered all of this before in the previous sections. We are just combining it all together. Now, we're done. I'm sure there are going to be errors, because there's quite a lot of code in here, so we'll get to that when we start compiling it. So let's just save it.

Now we will move on to our main code to make modifications to it.

Changes to the main code

Follow the below mentioned steps to combine the light source in our code:

1. In `main.cpp`, we need the lamp shader, so we'll uncomment it. After `cubePositions`, because now we've got multiple point light positions, we're going to add `glm::vec3`, and this is going to be called `pointLightPositions[]`. We are going to add `glm::vec3();` in there, and for this, we are going to pass `0.7f`, `0.2f`, and `2.0f`. Duplicate this line of code, paste it four times, and make the following changes:

```
        // Positions of the point lights
        glm::vec3 pointLightPositions[] =
```

Types of light sources and combining of lights

```
    {
        glm::vec3( 0.7f, 0.2f, 2.0f ),
        glm::vec3( 2.3f, -3.3f, -4.0f ),
        glm::vec3( -4.0f, 2.0f, -12.0f ),
        glm::vec3( 0.0f, 0.0f, -3.0f )
    };
```

2. Next, we'll uncomment the light vertex array object as we need it now to combine the lights.
3. The major changes that we need to make are within the `while` loop now. We're using the lighting shader, so we'll make the following changes to it:

    ```
    // Use cooresponding shader when setting uniforms/drawing objects
    lightingShader.Use( );
    GLint viewPosLoc = glGetUniformLocation( lightingShader.Program, "viewPos" );
    glUniform3f( viewPosLoc, camera.GetPosition( ).x, camera.GetPosition( ).y, camera.GetPosition( ).z);
    // Set material properties
    glUniform1f( glGetUniformLocation( lightingShader.Program, "material.shininess" ), 32.0f );
    ```

4. We're setting the uniforms for the directional light:

    ```
    // Directional light
    glUniform3f( glGetUniformLocation( lightingShader.Program, "dirLight.direction" ), -0.2f, -1.0f, -0.3f );
    glUniform3f( glGetUniformLocation( lightingShader.Program, "dirLight.ambient" ), 0.05f, 0.05f, 0.05f );
    glUniform3f( glGetUniformLocation( lightingShader.Program, "dirLight.diffuse" ), 0.4f, 0.4f, 0.4f );
    glUniform3f( glGetUniformLocation( lightingShader.Program, "dirLight.specular" ), 0.5f, 0.5f, 0.5f );
    ```

5. Then we'll set the uniforms for point light 1:

    ```
    // Point light 1
    glUniform3f( glGetUniformLocation( lightingShader.Program, "pointLights[0].position" ), pointLightPositions[0].x, pointLightPositions[0].y, pointLightPositions[0].z );
    glUniform3f( glGetUniformLocation( lightingShader.Program, "pointLights[0].ambient" ), 0.05f, 0.05f, 0.05f );
    glUniform3f( glGetUniformLocation( lightingShader.Program, "pointLights[0].diffuse" ), 0.8f, 0.8f, 0.8f );
    glUniform3f( glGetUniformLocation( lightingShader.Program, "pointLights[0].specular" ), 1.0f, 1.0f, 1.0f );
    glUniform1f( glGetUniformLocation( lightingShader.Program, "pointLights[0].constant" ), 1.0f );
    ```

```
    glUniform1f( glGetUniformLocation( lightingShader.Program,
"pointLights[0].linear" ), 0.09f );
    glUniform1f( glGetUniformLocation( lightingShader.Program,
"pointLights[0].quadratic" ), 0.032f );
```

6. Similarly, set the uniforms for point light 2:

```
// Point light 2
    glUniform3f( glGetUniformLocation( lightingShader.Program,
"pointLights[1].position" ), pointLightPositions[1].x,
pointLightPositions[1].y, pointLightPositions[1].z );
    glUniform3f( glGetUniformLocation( lightingShader.Program,
"pointLights[1].ambient" ), 0.05f, 0.05f, 0.05f );
    glUniform3f( glGetUniformLocation( lightingShader.Program,
"pointLights[1].diffuse" ), 0.8f, 0.8f, 0.8f );
    glUniform3f( glGetUniformLocation( lightingShader.Program,
"pointLights[1].specular" ), 1.0f, 1.0f, 1.0f );
    glUniform1f( glGetUniformLocation( lightingShader.Program,
"pointLights[1].constant" ), 1.0f );
    glUniform1f( glGetUniformLocation( lightingShader.Program,
"pointLights[1].linear" ), 0.09f );
    glUniform1f( glGetUniformLocation( lightingShader.Program,
"pointLights[1].quadratic" ), 0.032f );
```

7. Here are the definition of the uniforms for point light 3:

```
// Point light 3
    glUniform3f( glGetUniformLocation( lightingShader.Program,
"pointLights[2].position" ), pointLightPositions[2].x,
pointLightPositions[2].y, pointLightPositions[2].z );
    glUniform3f( glGetUniformLocation( lightingShader.Program,
"pointLights[2].ambient" ), 0.05f, 0.05f, 0.05f );
    glUniform3f( glGetUniformLocation( lightingShader.Program,
"pointLights[2].diffuse" ), 0.8f, 0.8f, 0.8f );
    glUniform3f( glGetUniformLocation( lightingShader.Program,
"pointLights[2].specular" ), 1.0f, 1.0f, 1.0f );
    glUniform1f( glGetUniformLocation( lightingShader.Program,
"pointLights[2].constant" ), 1.0f );
    glUniform1f( glGetUniformLocation( lightingShader.Program,
"pointLights[2].linear" ), 0.09f );
    glUniform1f( glGetUniformLocation( lightingShader.Program,
"pointLights[2].quadratic" ), 0.032f );
```

8. Here are the definitions for point light 4:

```
// Point light 4
    glUniform3f( glGetUniformLocation( lightingShader.Program,
"pointLights[3].position" ), pointLightPositions[3].x,
```

Types of light sources and combining of lights

```
pointLightPositions[3].y, pointLightPositions[3].z );
 glUniform3f( glGetUniformLocation( lightingShader.Program,
"pointLights[3].ambient" ), 0.05f, 0.05f, 0.05f );
 glUniform3f( glGetUniformLocation( lightingShader.Program,
"pointLights[3].diffuse" ), 0.8f, 0.8f, 0.8f );
 glUniform3f( glGetUniformLocation( lightingShader.Program,
"pointLights[3].specular" ), 1.0f, 1.0f, 1.0f );
 glUniform1f( glGetUniformLocation( lightingShader.Program,
"pointLights[3].constant" ), 1.0f );
 glUniform1f( glGetUniformLocation( lightingShader.Program,
"pointLights[3].linear" ), 0.09f );
 glUniform1f( glGetUniformLocation( lightingShader.Program,
"pointLights[3].quadratic" ), 0.032f );
```

9. Then we'll define uniforms for the spotlight as follows:

```
// SpotLight
 glUniform3f( glGetUniformLocation( lightingShader.Program,
"spotLight.position" ), camera.GetPosition( ).x,
camera.GetPosition( ).y, camera.GetPosition( ).z );
 glUniform3f( glGetUniformLocation( lightingShader.Program,
"spotLight.direction" ), camera.GetFront( ).x, camera.GetFront(
).y, camera.GetFront( ).z );

glUniform3f( glGetUniformLocation( lightingShader.Program,
"spotLight.ambient" ), 0.0f, 0.0f, 0.0f );

glUniform3f( glGetUniformLocation( lightingShader.Program,
"spotLight.diffuse" ), 1.0f, 1.0f, 1.0f );

glUniform3f( glGetUniformLocation( lightingShader.Program,
"spotLight.specular" ), 1.0f, 1.0f, 1.0f );

 glUniform1f( glGetUniformLocation( lightingShader.Program,
"spotLight.constant" ), 1.0f );

 glUniform1f( glGetUniformLocation( lightingShader.Program,
"spotLight.linear" ), 0.09f );

glUniform1f( glGetUniformLocation( lightingShader.Program,
"spotLight.quadratic" ), 0.032f );

glUniform1f( glGetUniformLocation( lightingShader.Program,
"spotLight.cutOff" ), glm::cos( glm::radians( 12.5f ) ) );
 glUniform1f( glGetUniformLocation( lightingShader.Program,
"spotLight.outerCutOff" ), glm::cos( glm::radians( 15.0f ) ) );
```

In the preceding lines of code, we set all the uniforms for the 5 or 6 types of lights we have. We have to set them manually and index the proper `PointLight` struct in the array to set each uniform variable. This can be made more code-friendly by defining light types as classes and setting their values in there, or by using a more efficient uniform approach by using uniform buffer objects.

10. We've still got all of the code that we don't need anymore, so, from just below the point where we finished our spotlight stuff to the point where we start defining our view matrix, we need to get rid of that all that code. These are the remnants from when we only had one type of light, and it was called `Light`, so we'll get rid of that.
11. We need to comment back in the shader, and I need to comment back in the deleting of the light vertex array object.
12. We've looped through our box array, we have created all the different boxes, and we've got our lamp shader. Remember, we've got multiple point lights, so we just need to create a loop for that. So, after binding the vertex array and unbinding it, we need to add `glBindVertexArray( lightVAO );`.
13. Then we'll add our `for` loop and pass the initializing parameters for the loop as `GLuint i = 0; i < 4; i++`, and to the loop we're going to add, `model = glm:: mat4();`.
14. Then, on the other line, we are going to add `model = glm::translate();`, and this is just going to be translating the `model`. And then the vector for this is going to be `pointLightPositions`. Then pass the iterator `[i]`.
15. And now, we're just going to make the cube a little bit smaller, as we have done before. So we'll add `model = glm::scale();`, and to that we are going to pass `model` and `glm::vec3( 0.2f )`.
16. On the other line we're going to add `glUniformMatrix4fv()` because it's a 4x4 matrix, and to that, we need to pass `modelLoc, 1, GL_FALSE;`, and `glm:: value_ptr();` to this, we are going to pass the model.
17. Then we'll add `glDrawArrays();`, and to that, we'll pass `GL_TRIANGLES, 0,` and `36`. And, after this for loop is completed on the other line, we need to unbind the vertex array as `glBindVertexArray( 0 );`. Take a look at the following code to understand the description:

```
// We now draw as many light bulbs as we have point lights.
glBindVertexArray( lightVAO );
for ( GLuint i = 0; i < 4; i++ )
{
model = glm::mat4( );
model = glm::translate( model, pointLightPositions[i] );
model = glm::scale( model, glm::vec3( 0.2f ) ); // Make it a
```

Types of light sources and combining of lights

```
        smaller cube
        glUniformMatrix4fv( modelLoc, 1, GL_FALSE, glm::value_ptr( model )
);
        glDrawArrays( GL_TRIANGLES, 0, 36 );
        }
        glBindVertexArray( 0 );
```

We are now all set to run the code. Save the updated code and compile it. You will get output similar to the following on your screen:

We've got our multiple light sources, four of which are point lights and one of which is just a regular lamp. We recommend you figure out which ones are the point lights and which one is the lamp. As you can see, we have the spotlight that is attached, and we also have the general directional light. You might be thinking that it's hard to tell which light is which, and generally, in the real world, it's hard to tell too. Light has an effect on everything around us, and this is how it works in the game. Now if you try to go further away from the object, our spotlight really isn't affecting the cube anymore, but it's still there, as seen in the following screenshot:

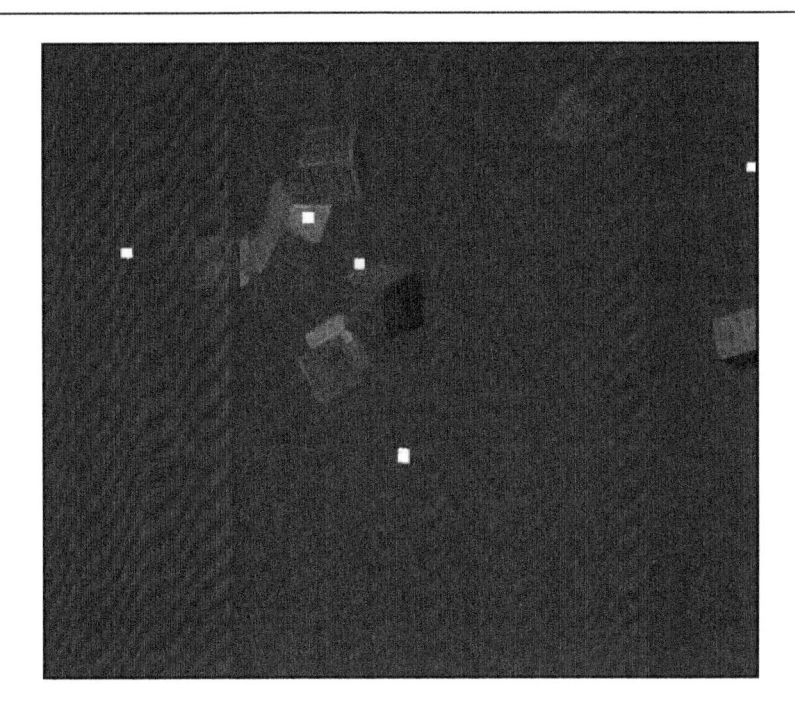

As we get closer to it, it starts affecting the object:

It's cool to see how the effect is combined with the other light sources. So, that's it for combining directional lights, point lights, and spotlights. There is a lot of lengthy code in this chapter, but a lot of it we've already done before.

Summary

In this chapter, we discussed about the different types of light sources such as directional, point and spotlight. Then we learned how to combine these light source and the lighting effects to generate realistic lighting in our game world.

In the next chapter, we'll discuss about the cube maps and we'll learn to generate the skybox using for our game.

6
Implementing a Skybox Using a Cubemap

In this chapter, we'll create a skybox using a cubemap. So, let's first understand what a cubemap is. It is a combination of multiple textures combined into a single texture, which is a cube. It is basically a series of six individual 2D textures that are mapped to a cube. They usually would have some sort of pattern to them, in a way that they actually flow from one side to the other. A skybox is essentially a cubemap, but a massive one. The player and the game world is essentially within that big cube. It encompasses the entire scene with six images of the game environment; if you, as a player, are inside a skybox and you try to look around, it would feel like you have a high-resolution world around you. And, if you try to reach for the edges of the cube you wouldn't be able to do that, because it's just infinitely far away from you. In this chapter, we'll learn how to implement a skybox using a cubemap to create amazing worlds within your game

We'll start by creating shaders for our Skybox.

> You can refer to all the code files for this chapter in the Chapter06 folder on GitHub. The GitHub link can be found in the preface of the book.

Creating shaders for the skybox

As usual, we'll begin with creating our shaders. We'll initiate by duplicating our shader files, `core.vs`, and `core.frag`, and name those copied files as `skybox.vs` and `skybox.frag`. We'll now carry out some modification on these shader files; take a look at the following steps to understand the changes that will be made:

1. We'll begin with making modifications to our `skybox.vs` shader. Take a look at the following code and implement the following modification in your shader file:

   ```
   #version 330 core

   layout (location = 0) in vec3 position;

   out vec3 TexCoords;
   uniform mat4 projection;
   uniform mat4 view;
   void main()

   {
       vec4 pos = projection * view * vec4(position, 1.0);
       gl_Position = pos.xyww;
       TexCoords = position;
   }
   ```

   Once you have made the changes, save the file.

2. Next, we'll move on to `Skybox.frag` and carry out the following highlighted changes to the code:

   ```
   #version 330 core
   in vec3 TexCoords;
   out vec4 color;
   uniform samplerCube skybox;
   void main()
   {
       color = texture(skybox, TexCoords);
   }
   ```

Save these changes to your shaders.

Now we have modified our shader files to implement the skybox, we'll move on to make modifications to our `main.cpp` file and create our skybox.

Modifications to the main.cpp file

In the `main.cpp` file, there are a few changes we need to make. Follow the steps shown here:

1. First of all, we need to create a new shader object, so before we define `GLfloat cubeVertices[]`, we need to add `Shader skyboxShader()`. And, to that we'll pass the locations of our shader files: `"res/shaders/skybox.vs"` and `"res/shaders/skybox.frag"`.
2. Next, we're going to need some more vertices for the skybox. Luckily, you can refer those to the `main.cpp` file present inside the `advanced_opengl` folder. Add these vertices to our code.
3. Once you've got the skybox vertices all set up, you will need to create a vertex array object and vertex buffer object for the skybox. So, let's do that right now.
4. After we have defined `glBindVertexArray(0)`, we'll add `GLuint skyboxVAO` and `skyboxVBO;`.
5. Then, we'll add `glGenVertexArrays();` the vertex array is going to take the parameter `1` and then a skybox vertex array object, `skyboxVAO`. Next, we're going to generate the buffers into the skybox vertex buffer object.
6. So, we'll add `glGenBuffers();` and to that we'll pass the parameter as `1` and `&skyboxVBO`.
7. Then add `glBindVertexArray()`, and to that we'll pass `skyboxVAO`.
8. Next, we add `glBindBuffer()`, and for this we'll pass `GL_ARRAY_BUFFER` and `skyboxVBO`. It's very similar to what we've already done before in the previous chapters, so all of this should be very familiar.
9. Add `glBufferData()`, and the first parameter it will take here is `GL_ARRAY_BUFFER`, and the size of the skybox vertices array. Next, we need to actually pass in `skyboxVertices`, and finally, we're just going to set it to `GL_STATIC_DRAW`.

Implementing a Skybox Using a Cubemap

10. Then we'll add `GLEnableVertexAttribArray()`. We're going to set this to 0. Next, we're going to add `glVertexAttribPointer()`. This is going to take 0, 3, GL_FLOAT, GL_FALSE, 3 * sizeof(GLfloat), (GLvoid *) 0. Take a look at the following code to understand the description:

```
// Setup skybox VAO
GLuint skyboxVAO, skyboxVBO;
glGenVertexArrays( 1, &skyboxVAO );
glGenBuffers( 1, &skyboxVBO );
glBindVertexArray( skyboxVAO );
glBindBuffer( GL_ARRAY_BUFFER, skyboxVBO );
glBufferData( GL_ARRAY_BUFFER, sizeof( skyboxVertices ),
&skyboxVertices, GL_STATIC_DRAW );
glEnableVertexAttribArray( 0 );
glVertexAttribPointer( 0, 3, GL_FLOAT, GL_FALSE, 3 * sizeof(
GLfloat ), ( GLvoid * ) 0 );
glBindVertexArray(0);
```

Creating the Texture.h file

Next, we will actually load the textures, so what we're going to do is create a separate texture file, and we'll just have a method for loading the textures, and also a separate method for loading cube textures. The reason for doing this is we're going to be using this code regularly, and it's just that we have to rewrite these every single time. If we want to do multiple objects, especially, we don't want to rewrite this every single time. Let's take a look at the following steps to create the `Texture.h` file:

1. First of all, we'll create an empty header file and name that as `Texture.h`, and add that to our project.
2. Then, in `Texture.h`, we'll add the following code:

   `#pragma once`

3. Then, we'll add some header files, such as `#define GLEW_STATIC` (if you didn't statically link GLEW, then you don't need to put this line here), `#include <GL/glew.h>`, and `#include <vector>`.
4. Next, we'll create a class called `TextureLoading` and begin adding all our code to it.
5. We'll type `public`, and the first method we're going to have is a `static GLuint LoadTexture()` and to that we'll pass `GLchar *path`.

6. Now, we'll go to our `main.cpp` file, and we'll cut and paste all the load and create textures and texture loading-related code, and paste it into the `LoadTextureMethod` that we created in the previous step.
7. Now, let's have a look at what we need to change in here; check out the following highlighted code to understand the changes:

```
static GLuint LoadTexture( GLchar *path )
{
    //Generate texture ID and load texture data
    GLuint textureID;
    glGenTextures( 1, &textureID );
    int imageWidth, imageHeight;
    unsigned char *image = SOIL_load_image( path, &imageWidth,
    &imageHeight, 0, SOIL_LOAD_RGB );
    // Assign texture to ID
    glBindTexture( GL_TEXTURE_2D, textureID );
    glTexImage2D( GL_TEXTURE_2D, 0, GL_RGB, imageWidth,
    imageHeight, 0, GL_RGB, GL_UNSIGNED_BYTE, image );
    glGenerateMipmap( GL_TEXTURE_2D );

    // Parameters
    glTexParameteri( GL_TEXTURE_2D, GL_TEXTURE_WRAP_S,
    GL_REPEAT );
    glTexParameteri( GL_TEXTURE_2D, GL_TEXTURE_WRAP_T,
    GL_REPEAT );
    glTexParameteri( GL_TEXTURE_2D, GL_TEXTURE_MIN_FILTER,
    GL_LINEAR_MIPMAP_LINEAR );
    glTexParameteri( GL_TEXTURE_2D, GL_TEXTURE_MAG_FILTER,
    GL_LINEAR );
    glBindTexture( GL_TEXTURE_2D, 0);
    SOIL_free_image_data( image );
    return textureID;
}

static GLuint LoadCubemap( vector<const GLchar * > faces)
{
    GLuint textureID;
    glGenTextures( 1, &textureID );
    int imageWidth, imageHeight;
    unsigned char *image;
        glBindTexture( GL_TEXTURE_CUBE_MAP, textureID );
    for ( GLuint i = 0; i < faces.size( ); i++ )
    {
        image = SOIL_load_image( faces[i], &imageWidth,
        &imageHeight, 0, SOIL_LOAD_RGB );
        glTexImage2D( GL_TEXTURE_CUBE_MAP_POSITIVE_X + i, 0,
        GL_RGB, imageWidth, imageHeight, 0, GL_RGB,
```

```
                GL_UNSIGNED_BYTE, image );
                SOIL_free_image_data( image );
        }
    glTexParameteri( GL_TEXTURE_CUBE_MAP, GL_TEXTURE_MAG_FILTER,
    GL_LINEAR );
    glTexParameteri( GL_TEXTURE_CUBE_MAP, GL_TEXTURE_MIN_FILTER,
    GL_LINEAR );
    glTexParameteri( GL_TEXTURE_CUBE_MAP, GL_TEXTURE_WRAP_S,
    GL_CLAMP_TO_EDGE );
    glTexParameteri( GL_TEXTURE_CUBE_MAP, GL_TEXTURE_WRAP_T,
    GL_CLAMP_TO_EDGE );
    glTexParameteri( GL_TEXTURE_CUBE_MAP, GL_TEXTURE_WRAP_R,
    GL_CLAMP_TO_EDGE );
    glBindTexture( GL_TEXTURE_CUBE_MAP, 0);
    return textureID;

}
```

8. Now, we go back to `main.cpp`, and add `#include Texture.h`, then come to the location in the code where we want to load textures, and there we'll add the following to load our texture code: `GLuint cubeTexture = TextureLoading::LoadTexture( "res/images/container2.png" )` and also update the bind texture code, as highlighted here:

```
glBindTexture( GL_TEXTURE_2D, cubeTexture );
```

Now, let's run it and check if our `Texture.h` code builds successfully, and that it compiles without any errors. You should get the following output on your screen:

Chapter 6

This isn't the cubemap at the moment, as we were just sorting out the texturing, but making a separate texture will allow us to easily reuse texture loading.

Adding cube mapping code to Texture.h

So now, what we actually want to do is essentially the similar process as we did with the texture file, but for cube mapping. The code will be very similar, so to begin with what we are going to do is duplicate the texture loading code and paste below it. Then, we'll make the following highlighted changes to the code:

```
static GLuint LoadCubemap( vector<const GLchar * > faces)
{
    GLuint textureID;
    glGenTextures( 1, &textureID );
    int imageWidth, imageHeight;
    unsigned char *image;
    glBindTexture( GL_TEXTURE_CUBE_MAP, textureID );
    for ( GLuint i = 0; i < faces.size( ); i++ )
    {
        image = SOIL_load_image( faces[i], &imageWidth, &imageHeight,
        0, SOIL_LOAD_RGB );
        glTexImage2D( GL_TEXTURE_CUBE_MAP_POSITIVE_X + i, 0, GL_RGB,
        imageWidth, imageHeight, 0, GL_RGB, GL_UNSIGNED_BYTE, image );
        SOIL_free_image_data( image );
    }

    glTexParameteri( GL_TEXTURE_CUBE_MAP, GL_TEXTURE_MAG_FILTER,
    GL_LINEAR );

    glTexParameteri( GL_TEXTURE_CUBE_MAP, GL_TEXTURE_MIN_FILTER,
    GL_LINEAR );

    glTexParameteri( GL_TEXTURE_CUBE_MAP, GL_TEXTURE_WRAP_S,
    GL_CLAMP_TO_EDGE );

    glTexParameteri( GL_TEXTURE_CUBE_MAP, GL_TEXTURE_WRAP_T,
    GL_CLAMP_TO_EDGE );

    glTexParameteri( GL_TEXTURE_CUBE_MAP, GL_TEXTURE_WRAP_R,
    GL_CLAMP_TO_EDGE );

    glBindTexture( GL_TEXTURE_CUBE_MAP, 0);
    return textureID;
}
```

Implementing a Skybox Using a Cubemap

In the preceding code, we added `GLchars` because we don't have one path; remember, we're going to have six different paths. Then, we created the `for` loop because we wanted to go over our six different images with ease, and also we didn't want to repeat the code, which was the whole point of doing what we're doing.

So, if we go back to our main file that is in our `main.cpp`, we can actually finish off what we were doing. Go to the section where we are loading our texture file, and after that code, add the following highlighted code:

```
// Cubemap (Skybox)

    vector<const GLchar*> faces;
    faces.push_back( "res/images/skybox/right.tga" );
    faces.push_back( "res/images/skybox/left.tga" );
    faces.push_back( "res/images/skybox/top.tga" );
    faces.push_back( "res/images/skybox/bottom.tga" );
    faces.push_back( "res/images/skybox/back.tga" );
    faces.push_back( "res/images/skybox/front.tga" );
    GLuint cubemapTexture = TextureLoading::LoadCubemap( faces )
```

In the preceding code, we added the cubemap texture. The order here does matter, so you can't just willy-nilly put it in. If you downloaded other images from a website, you might need to rearrange it properly.

Drawing the skybox

Now, what we need to actually do is, well, draw the skybox, so let's begin by following the steps shown here:

1. Go to the location in our code where we're done with all the model matrix stuff, and we're going to add `glDepthFunc()`; and in there, we need to pass `GL_LEQUAL`. This changes the depth function, so the depth test passes when values are equal to the depth buffer's content.
2. Next, we're going to add `skyboxShader.Use()`.
3. Then, add `view = glmm::mat4()`. And in here, we are going to pass `glm::mat3()`, and to that we'll pass `camera.GetViewMatrix()`.
4. Next, add `glUniformMatrix4fv()`. For this, we will pass the following: `glGetUniformLocation( skyboxShader.Program, "view" ), 1, GL_FALSE, glm::value_ptr( view )`.

5. We need to do something very similar for the projection matrix as well. So, we will add the following code: `glUniformMatrix4fv( glGetUniformLocation( skyboxShader.Program, "projection" ), 1, GL_FALSE, glm::value_ptr( projection ) );`.
6. Now what we need to do is just add the skybox cube. So, add `glBindVertexArray();` function and to that we'll pass `skyboxVAO`, and then add `glBindTexture()`. And for the bind texture function, it's going to be `GL_TEXTURE_CUBE_MAP`. Then, add the `cubemapTexture` that we call the `LoadCubemap` method.
7. Then, add `glDrawArrays();`. And, the parameters we'll pass are as follows: `GL_TRIANGLES, 0, 36`. Again, this is just a cube, so it's very simple stuff.
8. Next, add `glBindVertexArray()`. For that, pass 0, as we normally would.
9. Now, we just need to set the `glDepthFunc()` back, and to that we're going to pass `GL_LESS`; this just sets it back to default.

And now, we should be ready to run, so let's run this and check what output we get on the screen. We should get the following scene:

It literally does look like we've created a 3D world. If you try moving away, you can see the cube getting smaller and smaller. But, everything else is staying the same because we're going to be infinitely far away from all of the sides.

Implementing a Skybox Using a Cubemap

Summary

In this chapter, we generated a Skybox using a cubemap, and learned to apply various textures to it. We also learned how to create the separate texture file to load our textures in the code. Also, we learned how to draw the skybox and created our game world using it.

There's a bonus chapter for you on Model Loading on the following link: `https://www.packtpub.com/sites/default/files/downloads/ModelLoading.pdf`

In this chapter, you'll learn how to setup Assimp (Open Asset Import Library) on Windows using CMake for all our Model Loading needs. You'll also get to learn how to create mesh class and Model class to handle loading of our model.

Other Books You May Enjoy

If you enjoyed this book, you may be interested in these other books by Packt:

OpenGL – Build high performance graphics
Muhammad Mobeen Movania, David Wolff, Raymond C. H. Lo, William C. Y. Lo

ISBN: 9781788296724

- Off-screen rendering and environment mapping techniques to render mirrors
- Shadow mapping techniques, including variance shadow mapping
- Implement a particle system using shaders
- Utilize noise in shaders
- Make use of compute shaders for physics, animation, and general computing
- Create interactive applications using GLFW to handle user inputs and the Android Sensor framework to detect gestures and motions on mobile devices
- Use OpenGL primitives to plot 2-D datasets (such as time series) dynamically
- Render complex 3D volumetric datasets with techniques such as data slicers and multiple viewpoint projection

Other Books You May Enjoy

Vulkan Cookbook
Pawel Lapinski

ISBN: 9781786468154

- Work with Swapchain to present images on screen
- Create, submit, and synchronize operations processed by the hardware
- Create buffers and images, manage their memory, and upload data to them from CPU
- Explore descriptor sets and set up an interface between application and shaders
- Organize drawing operations into a set of render passes and subpasses
- Prepare graphics pipelines to draw 3D scenes and compute pipelines to perform mathematical calculations
- Implement geometry projection and tessellation, texturing, lighting, and post-processing techniques
- Write shaders in GLSL and convert them into SPIR-V assemblies
- Find out about and implement a collection of popular, advanced rendering techniques found in games and benchmarks

Leave a review - let other readers know what you think

Please share your thoughts on this book with others by leaving a review on the site that you bought it from. If you purchased the book from Amazon, please leave us an honest review on this book's Amazon page. This is vital so that other potential readers can see and use your unbiased opinion to make purchasing decisions, we can understand what our customers think about our products, and our authors can see your feedback on the title that they have worked with Packt to create. It will only take a few minutes of your time, but is valuable to other potential customers, our authors, and Packt. Thank you!

Index

A
ambient lighting 124

C
Camera class
  adding, to project 94
  camera.h header file, creating 95, 97, 100, 102
  main.cpp, modifying 104, 106, 110
cube object
  adding 114
  code, modifying 116

D
diffuse lighting 125
directional light
  about 147, 148
  code changes, creating 150, 152
Dynamic Link Library (DLL) 20

G
GLM
  shader files, updating 79
  transformations, applying to objects 79, 82
  used, for setting up project on Windows/Mac 78
  used, for transformations 78

H
Homebrew
  about 21
  URL 21

L
light maps
  about 137
  code, changing 141, 143
  shader files, modifying 138, 140
  while loop, modifying 144, 145
light sources
  adding 114
  code, changing 175, 179, 181
  code, modifying 116
  combining 168
  directional light 168
  lamp shader files, creating 114
  lighting, creating 114
  point light 168
  shader files, obtaining 168, 170
  spotlight 168
  void main of lighting.frag, modifying 171, 173
lighting.frag shader
  updating 124

M
main.cpp file
  cube mapping code, adding to Texture.h 189
  modifications 185
  skybox, drawing 190
  texture.h file, creating 186
materials
  about 131
  code, changing 134, 137
  shader files, updating 132

N
normals 123

O
objects
  camera.h, changing 126
  code, changing 126, 129, 130, 131
  lighting up 122

shaders, updating 122
Open Graphics Library (OpenGL)
  about 7
  code, adding to draw shape 53
  DLL file, adding 35, 41
  rendering window, creating GLFW libraries used 24, 27, 29
  rendering window, creating SDL used 37, 39
  rendering window, creating SFML used 42, 44
  SDL library, downloading 30
  setting up, GLEW used on Windows 8
  setting up, GLEW used with relative linking 32
  setting up, GLFW libraries used on Mac 20
  setting up, GLFW used on Windows 8
  setting up, SDL used on Mac 35
  setting up, SDL used on Windows 30
  setting up, SDL used with absolute linking 31
  setting up, SDL used with relative linking 32
  setting up, SFML used on Mac 42
  setting up, SFML used on Windows 41
  triangle, drawing 46, 49, 51
  Xcode, setting up 22
  Xcode, setting up SDL used 36
OpenGL Extension Wrangler (GLEW)
  about 8, 30
  Dynamic Link Library (DLL), adding 20
  libraries, downloading 8, 35
  libraries, downloading for Mac 21
  libraries, linking with absolute linking 11, 14
  libraries, linking with relative linking 16, 18
  URL, for downloading 9
  used, for setting up OpenGL on Windows 8
OpenGL framework (GLFW)
  Dynamic Link Library (DLL), adding 20
  libraries, downloading 8
  libraries, downloading for Mac 21
  libraries, linking with absolute linking 11, 14
  libraries, linking with relative linking 16, 18
  used, for creating OpenGL rendering window 25, 27, 29
  used, for setting up OpenGL 20
  used, for setting up OpenGL on Windows 8
OpenGL framework
  URL 10

P

point light
  about 153
  attenuation section 155
  concept 153
  diffuse section 154
  main.cpp, changes creating 156, 159, 161
  specular section 155
projection and coordinate systems, code
  orthographic projection 91, 93
  View Frustum 87
  while loop, modifying 88
projection and coordinate systems
  about 82
  code, modifying 84, 85
  shader files, modifications creating 84

S

shader files
  creating, for lamp 115
shaders
  abstracting 55
  creating, for skybox 184
  draw triangle code, changes creating 60, 62
  files, creating 56
  Shader.h header file, creating 57, 58
simple and fast multimedia library (SFML)
  about 41
  GLEW library, linking 41
  library, downloading 41
  library, linking 41
  used, for creating OpenGL rendering window 42, 44
  used, for setting up OpenGL on Mac 42
  used, for setting up OpenGL on Windows 41
Simple DirectMedia Layer (SDL)
  about 30
  downloading 35
  used, for creating OpenGL rendering window 37, 39
  used, for setting up OpenGL on Mac 35
  used, for setting up Xcode 36
specular lighting 126
spotlight

[198]

about 161
  camera.h, modifying 164
  code changes, creating 164, 166
  shader files, changes creating 162

T

textures
  applying, to shape 63
  loading, to shape 63

V

vertex array object (VAO) 52
vertex buffer object (VBO) 52
Visual Studio Community 2017 8

W

while loop
  modifying 118, 120, 121

Printed in Great Britain
by Amazon